THE PLANETS

by Lisa Bullard

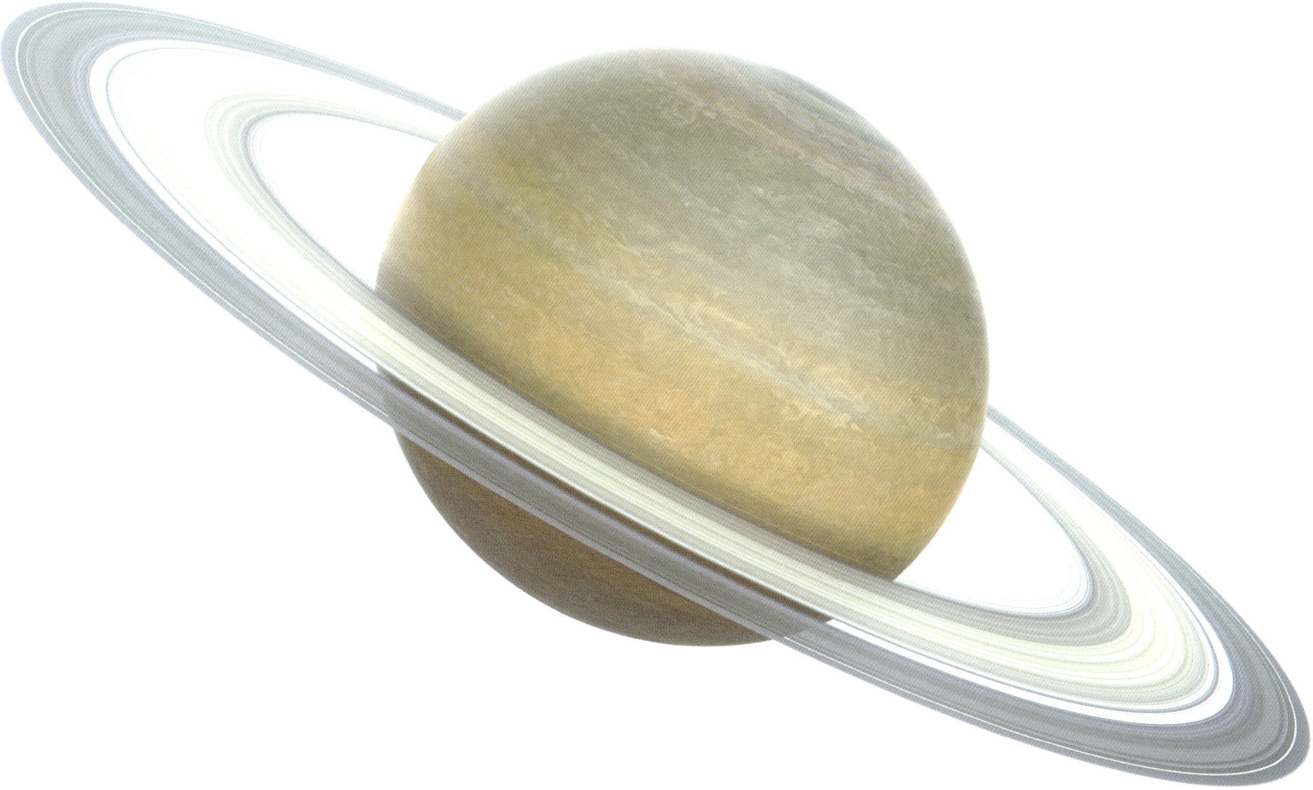

Early Encyclopedias

An Imprint of Abdo Reference
abdobooks.com

abdobooks.com

Published by Abdo Reference, a division of ABDO, PO Box 398166, Minneapolis, Minnesota 55439.

Printed in China.
102025
012026

Editor: Arnold Ringstad
Series Designers: Candice Keimig, Joshua Olson
Production Designer: Pat Maloney

Library of Congress Control Number: 2025939294

Publisher's Cataloging-in-Publication Data

Names: Bullard, Lisa, author.
Title: The planets / by Lisa Bullard
Description: Minneapolis, Minnesota: Abdo Reference, 2026 | Series: Early space encyclopedias | Includes online resources and index.
Identifiers: ISBN 9781098298807 (lib. bdg.) | ISBN 9798384932604 (ebook)
Subjects: LCSH: Outer space--Exploration--Juvenile literature. | Astronomy--Juvenile literature. | Solar System--Juvenile literature. | Planets--Juvenile literature. | Sky--Juvenile literature. | Encyclopedias--Juvenile literature.
Classification: DDC 523.4--dc23

CONTENTS

A star's powerful gravity holds planets in place.

Planets Travel around a Star

Planets are large objects in space. They orbit a star. Earth is a planet. It orbits around the star called the sun. The sun's gravity keeps Earth in orbit.

How Planets Are Born

New stars begin in clouds of gas and dust. Gravity pulls these things together. They get denser and hotter. A star forms. Leftover gas and dust become planets.

Planets Have Strong Gravity

Planets also have gravity. That gravity pulls at the things that make up the planet. It pulls toward the planet's center. The pull is strong because planets are big. It gives planets a rounded shape. Gravity also keeps a planet's orbit clear of similar-sized objects.

Gravity pulls large enough objects into a round shape.

Inner Planets

Eight planets orbit the sun. The closest four are called the inner planets. These are Mercury, Venus, Earth, and Mars. They are terrestrial planets. This means they are made mostly of rocks and metals.

Outer Planets

The four outer planets are much larger. They do not have solid surfaces. Jupiter and Saturn are called gas giants. They are big balls of gas. Uranus and Neptune are called ice giants. They are mostly made of ice.

First from the Sun

Mercury is the planet nearest to the sun. Sometimes it orbits as close as 29 million miles (47 million km). Sunlight reaches it in about three minutes.

Spacecraft have taken close-up pictures of Mercury.

How Mercury Got Its Name

Mercury can be seen in Earth's night sky. Humans have viewed the planet for thousands of years. People named the planet long ago. Mercury was the speedy messenger of the Roman gods.

Mercury's closeness to the sun gives it a fast orbital speed.

Orbit

Mercury's orbit is the fastest of the eight planets. It moves around the sun in 88 Earth days. It orbits in an egg shape. The other planets' orbits are more like circles.

FUN FACT!

Mercury moves almost 29 miles per second (47 km/s).

Rotation

Planets rotate, or spin, around an axis. It takes Mercury 59 Earth days to rotate once. Some planets are tilted on their axis. But Mercury has almost no tilt.

Mercury's lack of tilt means it has no seasons.

Planet Size

Mercury is the smallest planet in the solar system. The planet is slowly getting smaller over time. It is cooling down inside. As Mercury cools, it shrinks.

Mercury is slightly larger than Earth's moon.

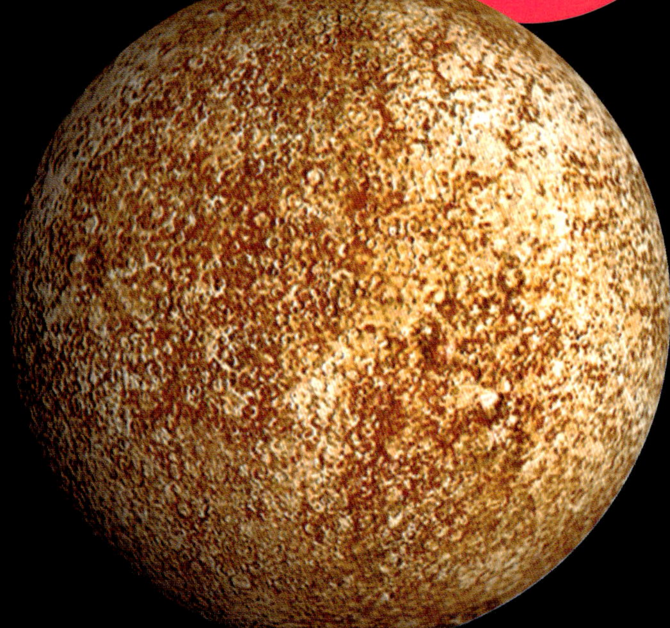

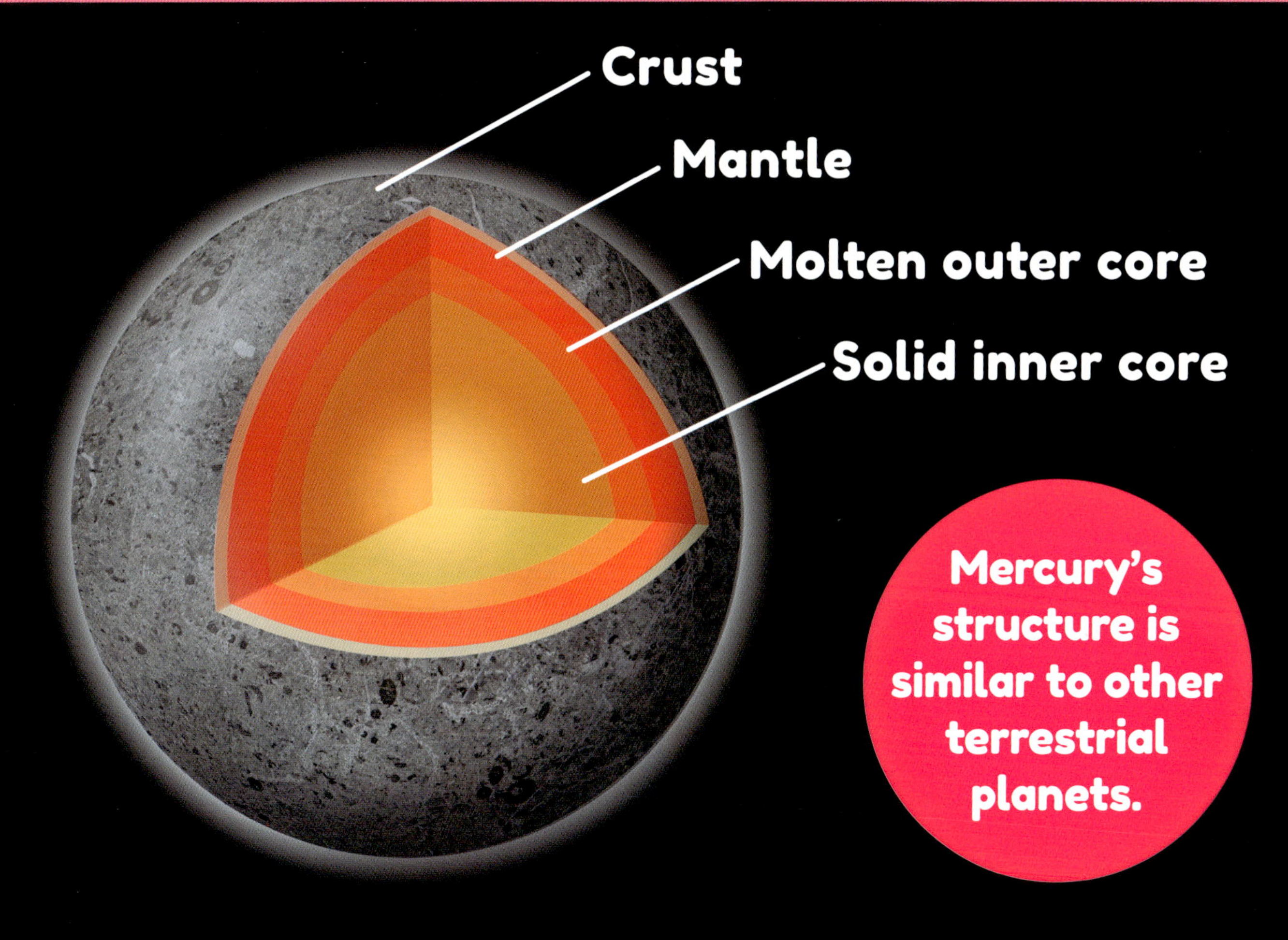

Structure

Terrestrial planets such as Mercury have three main layers. A core makes up the middle. Around that is the mantle. On top of that is the crust. Mercury's core makes up a huge part of the planet. It is mostly iron. That makes it very dense.

Mercury is a mostly airless world.

Atmosphere

Mercury's gravity is weak. It cannot hold an atmosphere. Mercury has only a thin exosphere. This thin layer of gas does not give Mercury much protection from the sun.

Weather

The sun is up to seven times brighter on Mercury than on Earth. Surface temperatures reach 800 degrees Fahrenheit (430°C). But there is no atmosphere to hold in heat. Nighttime drops to –290 degrees Fahrenheit (–180°C).

Night and day have big temperature differences on Mercury.

Mercury's surface has long cliffs.

On the Surface

Mercury has a rocky surface. It is covered by craters. This is because space rocks often hit the planet. Mercury has large cliffs. These formed as the planet cooled and shrank.

Ice Near the Sun

Scientists believe there may be ice at Mercury's poles. Sunlight never reaches the bottoms of deep craters there.

No Moons

Mercury has no moons. It is a small planet with weak gravity. And it is close to the sun. The sun's gravity is very strong. This means Mercury cannot hold onto a moon.

Scientists created an image showing temperatures at Mercury's north pole. Blue showed low temperatures. Deep craters were cooler than surrounding areas.

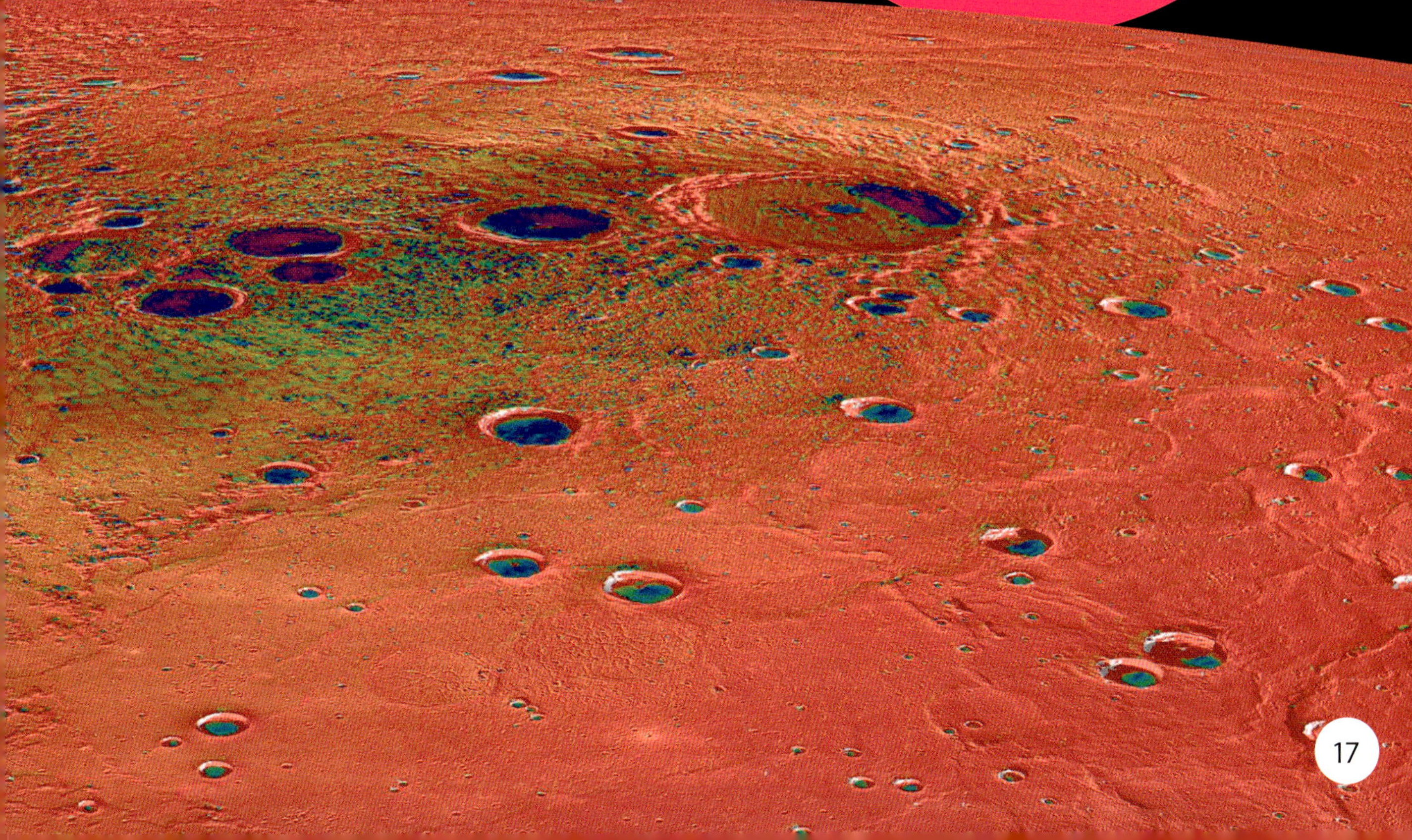

Why Explore Mercury?

It is hard to explore Mercury. The sun can harm telescopes pointed toward Mercury. The planet is close to the sun in the sky. Spacecraft must survive high heat near Mercury. But studying it helps scientists learn about other hot planets.

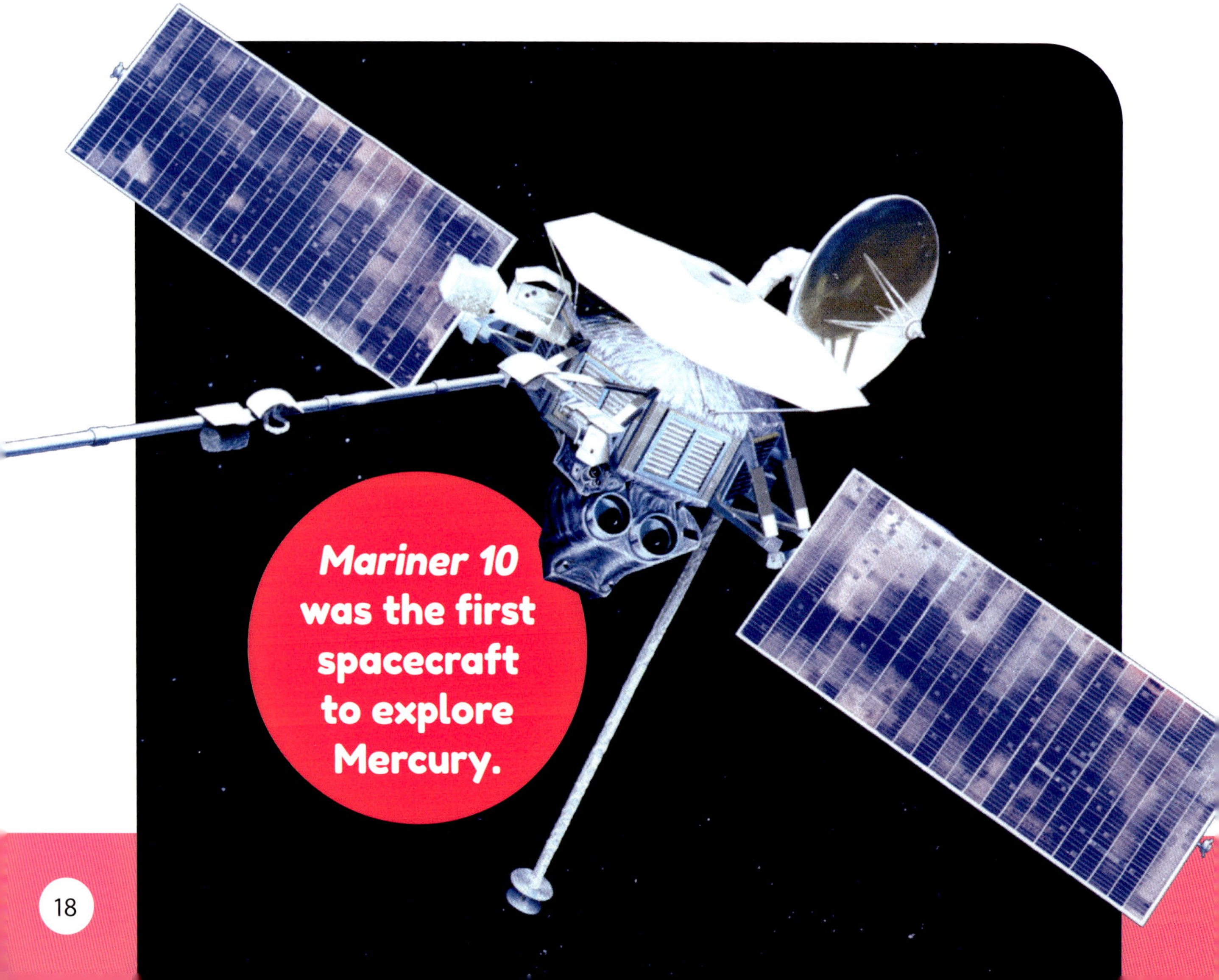

Mariner 10 **was the first spacecraft to explore Mercury.**

BepiColombo is run by space organizations from Europe and Japan.

Mercury Missions

Three spacecraft have explored Mercury. *Mariner 10* flew by three times in the 1970s. *MESSENGER* started a four-year orbit in 2011. *BepiColombo* launched in 2018.

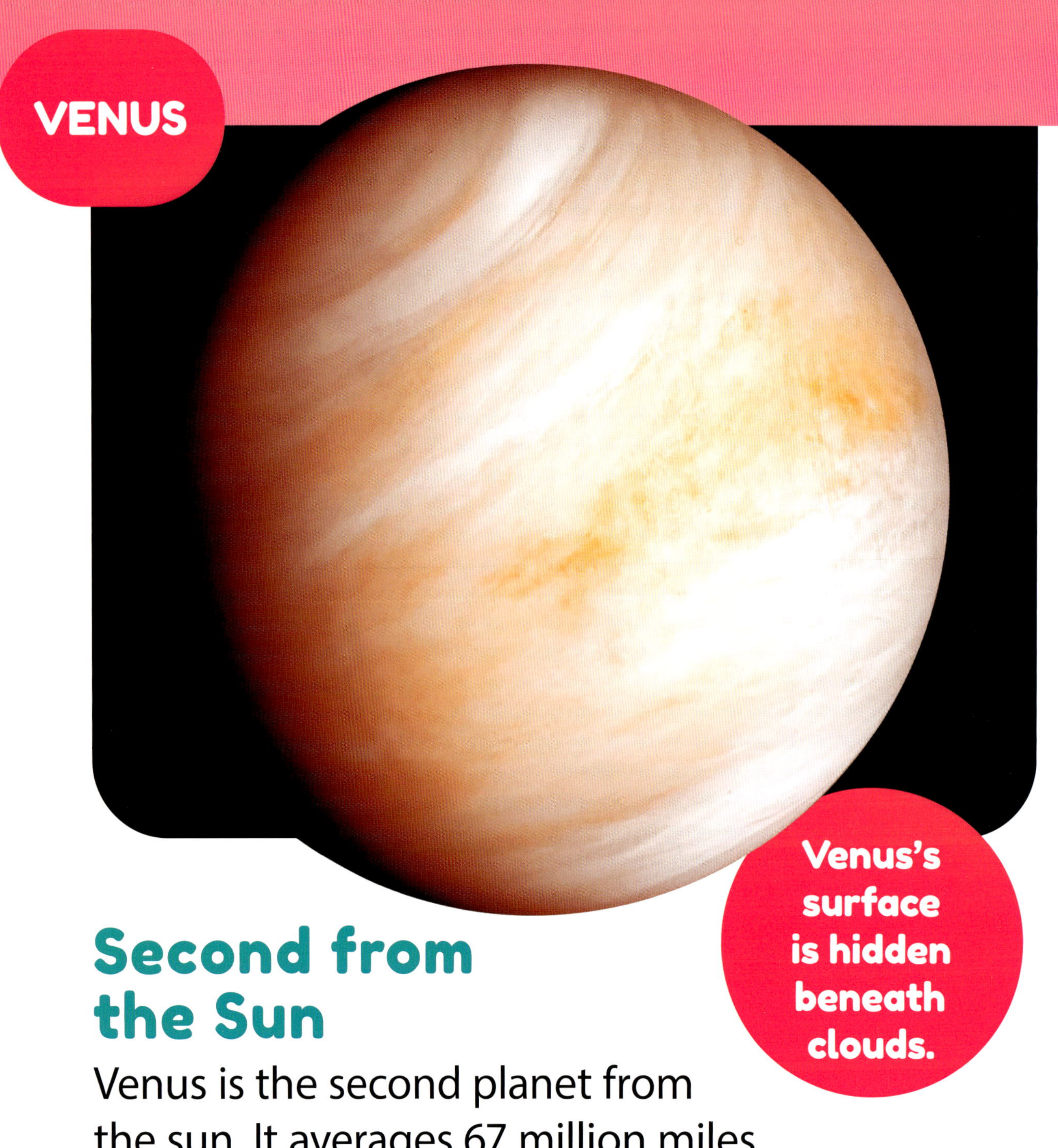

Venus's surface is hidden beneath clouds.

Second from the Sun

Venus is the second planet from the sun. It averages 67 million miles (108 million km) away from the sun. Sunlight reaches it in about six minutes. Mercury and Earth are Venus's neighbors.

How Venus Got Its Name

Humans have viewed Venus since early times. It is bright in the sky. Only the sun and the moon look brighter from Earth. Long ago, Venus was named for a Roman goddess. She stood for love and beauty.

Orbit

Venus orbits the sun in 225 Earth days. That is shorter than the time it takes to rotate. This means that on Venus, a year is shorter than a day.

Venus is millions of miles closer to the sun than Earth is.

How Long Is a Day?

This table shows the length of a day on each planet in Earth hours. Some planets have shorter days than Earth, and some have far longer ones.

Planet	Length of day
Mercury	1,408 hours
Venus	5,832 hours
Earth	24 hours
Mars	25 hours
Jupiter	10 hours
Saturn	11 hours
Uranus	17 hours
Neptune	16 hours

Rotation

Venus rotates very slowly. One rotation takes 243 Earth days. It goes clockwise. That is backward compared with most solar system planets. Venus has little tilt on its axis. It does not have seasons.

Earth

Venus is very similar to Earth in size.

Venus

Planet Size

Venus is the third-smallest planet in the solar system. It is bigger than Mercury and Mars. It is nearly Earth's size. Venus's diameter is just a few hundred miles smaller.

Structure

Venus is a terrestrial planet. Its inside is similar to Earth's. Venus has a mostly iron core. A thick, hot mantle surrounds that. A thin, rocky crust is on top. Volcanoes change the landscape.

Like other planets, Venus has a solid iron core.

An artist's illustration shows the deadly surface and atmosphere of Venus.

Atmosphere

Venus's atmosphere is very thick. It is made mostly of carbon dioxide. The high pressure would crush a person. Pale clouds surround the planet. The air on Venus is not safe for humans.

Weather

Venus is the hottest planet. Its atmosphere traps the sun's heat. Surface temperatures reach 867 degrees Fahrenheit (464°C). Venus also has strong winds.

FUN FACT!

Scientists believe sulfur in Venus's clouds makes the planet smell like rotten eggs.

Venus is as hot as the inside of a pizza oven.

Spacecraft can look through Venus's clouds to see its surface features.

On the Surface

The surface of Venus is very dry. Cooled lava covers much of the planet. There are high mountains. Some volcanoes are still active. Valleys and channels mark the surface too.

FUN FACT!

It is hot enough on the surface of Venus to melt lead.

A Quasi-Moon

Venus does not have a moon. A quasi-moon was discovered in 2002. It is named Zoozve. It stays near Venus. But it actually orbits the sun. Someday it may move away from Venus.

A Funny Mistake

When it was discovered, Zoozve was labeled "2002 VE68." Someone misread the numbers and letters as "ZOOZVE." Finally, the funny mistake became its official name.

Zoozve is just a few hundred meters wide.

Why Explore Venus?

Venus is sometimes called Earth's twin. Venus's atmosphere has much more carbon dioxide. But carbon dioxide is increasing in Earth's atmosphere. Studying Venus shows what this might mean for Earth.

Venus Missions

More than 40 missions have set out for Venus. Several of them failed. *Mariner 2* was the first to fly past Venus in 1962. The Soviet Union landed probes on the surface in the 1970s. New missions are being planned for the 2030s.

The *Venera* landers survived just long enough to send back data about Venus.

NASA sent the *Magellan* spacecraft to Venus in 1989.

Astronauts have taken photos of Earth from space.

Third from the Sun

Earth is the third planet from the sun. On average, it is 93 million miles (150 million km) away from its star. Sunlight reaches Earth in about eight minutes. Earth's neighbors are Venus and Mars.

How Earth Got Its Name

People have used many different names for Earth. Gaia was the Greek goddess of the earth. And la Tierra means "the Earth" in Spanish. The word *earth* basically means "the ground." It comes from Old English and Germanic.

FUN FACT!

Many ancient people believed that the sun orbited Earth.

The word *earth* is also used for soil.

Orbit

A calendar year is 365 days. But Earth orbits the sun in 365 and one-quarter days. This adds up to one extra day after four years. A day is added to the calendar every fourth year. It is called a leap day.

Earth's motion creates days and years.

Rotation

Earth rotates in just under 24 hours. The planet is tilted at about 23.5 degrees. That is why Earth has seasons. Sometimes the northern part of Earth tilts toward the sun. That is summer for that part of the globe. The southern part of Earth experiences winter at this time.

Planet Size

Earth is the fifth-biggest solar system planet. It is 7,926 miles (12,756 km) across the middle. Earth is the biggest inner planet. It is much smaller than the outer planets.

Structure

Earth is a terrestrial planet. It has inner and outer cores. They are made of iron and nickel. A thick mantle surrounds them. A rocky crust tops that. The outer part of Earth is divided into giant pieces. These are called tectonic plates.

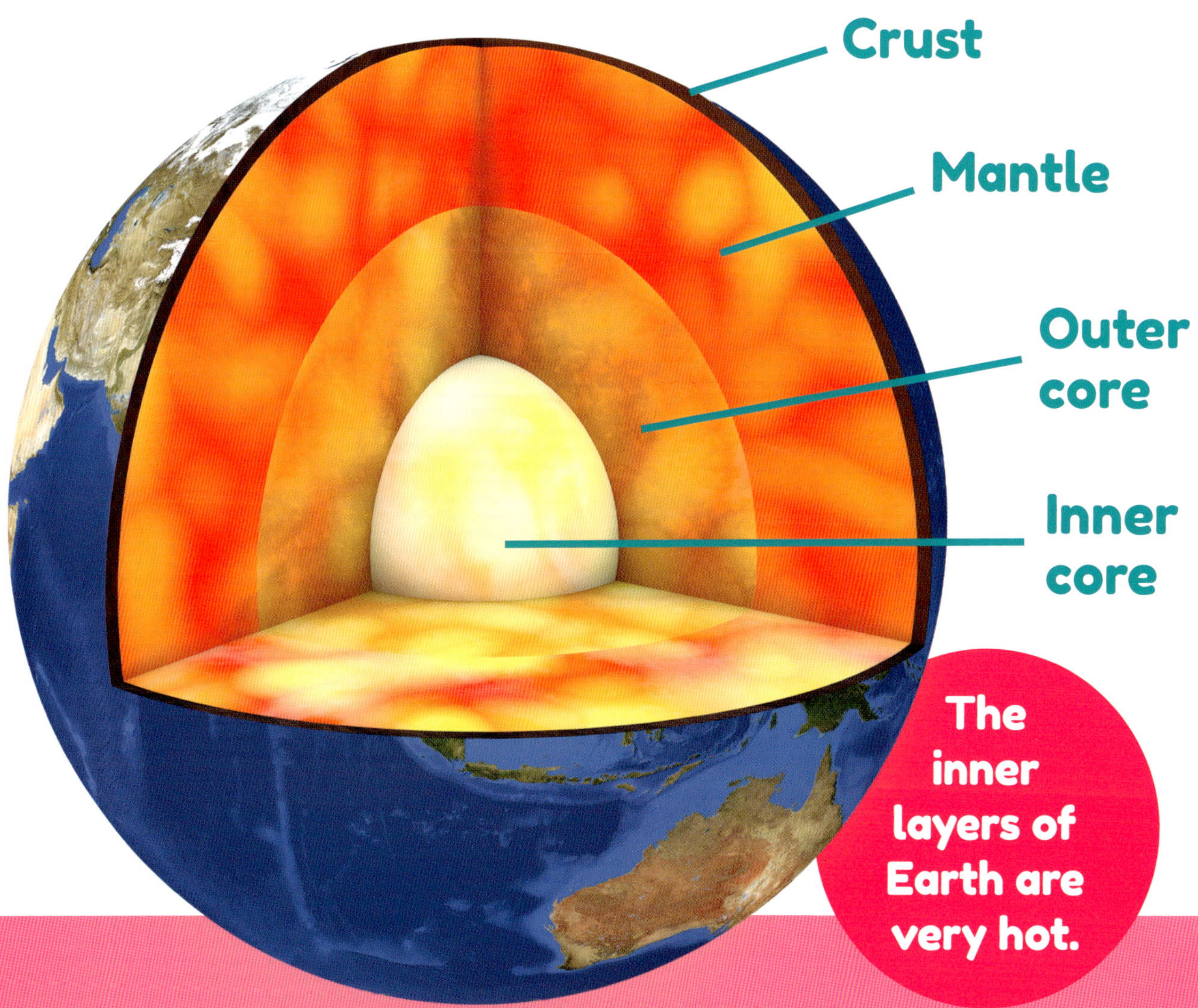

The inner layers of Earth are very hot.

Atmosphere

Nitrogen and oxygen make up most of Earth's atmosphere. People and animals breathe oxygen. Earth's atmosphere also blocks harmful energy from the sun.

Earth's thin atmosphere can be seen from space.

Weather

Earth's atmosphere traps some of the sun's heat. This keeps temperatures at a safe level for life. Earth's atmosphere also holds water vapor. This water forms clouds. It then falls to the ground as rain and snow. Water is important for life.

The Pacific Ocean covers a huge part of Earth's surface.

On the Surface

More than half of Earth is covered with oceans. No other planet has so much liquid water. Earth's tectonic plates move and shift. This shapes the planet. It forms mountains and valleys. It also causes earthquakes.

One Moon

Earth is the only solar system planet with one moon. On average, the moon is 238,855 miles (384,400 km) away. Scientists believe the moon was once part of Earth. But billions of years ago, a large object crashed into Earth. Chunks broke off and formed the moon.

The same side of the moon always faces Earth.

Why Protect Earth?

Earth is the only place in the solar system known to have life. The planet has water. It has safe temperatures. It has breathable air. It has a protective atmosphere. Living things need all of these. Caring for the planet keeps Earth livable.

Earth Missions

Many space missions study Earth. Spacecraft observe the oceans and air. Other missions have traveled to the moon. In 1969, humans landed there during the Apollo 11 mission. Future missions will return people to the moon's surface.

How Much Life?

More than 2 million living things have official names. But new ones are always being discovered. Nobody knows the true total number.

From the moon, Earth looks small in the sky.

Mars has many craters and other surface features.

Fourth from the Sun

Mars is the solar system's fourth planet. On average, it is 142 million miles (228 million km) from the sun. Sunlight takes 13 minutes to reach Mars. Mars and Earth are neighbors.

How Mars Got Its Name

Mars is easy to see in the sky. Early humans observed this red dot. People gave it a name long ago. Mars is the Roman god of war. The name fits the planet's red color.

People can see Mars with the naked eye. Telescopes offer an even better view.

Orbit

Mars orbits the sun in 687 Earth days. The planet's orbit is egg shaped like Mercury's. It moves closer to and farther from the sun through the year.

Mars's distance from the sun makes the planet's surface cold.

Rotation

Mars rotates more slowly than Earth. A day on Mars is about 40 minutes longer. Like Earth, Mars is tilted on its axis. It has seasons.

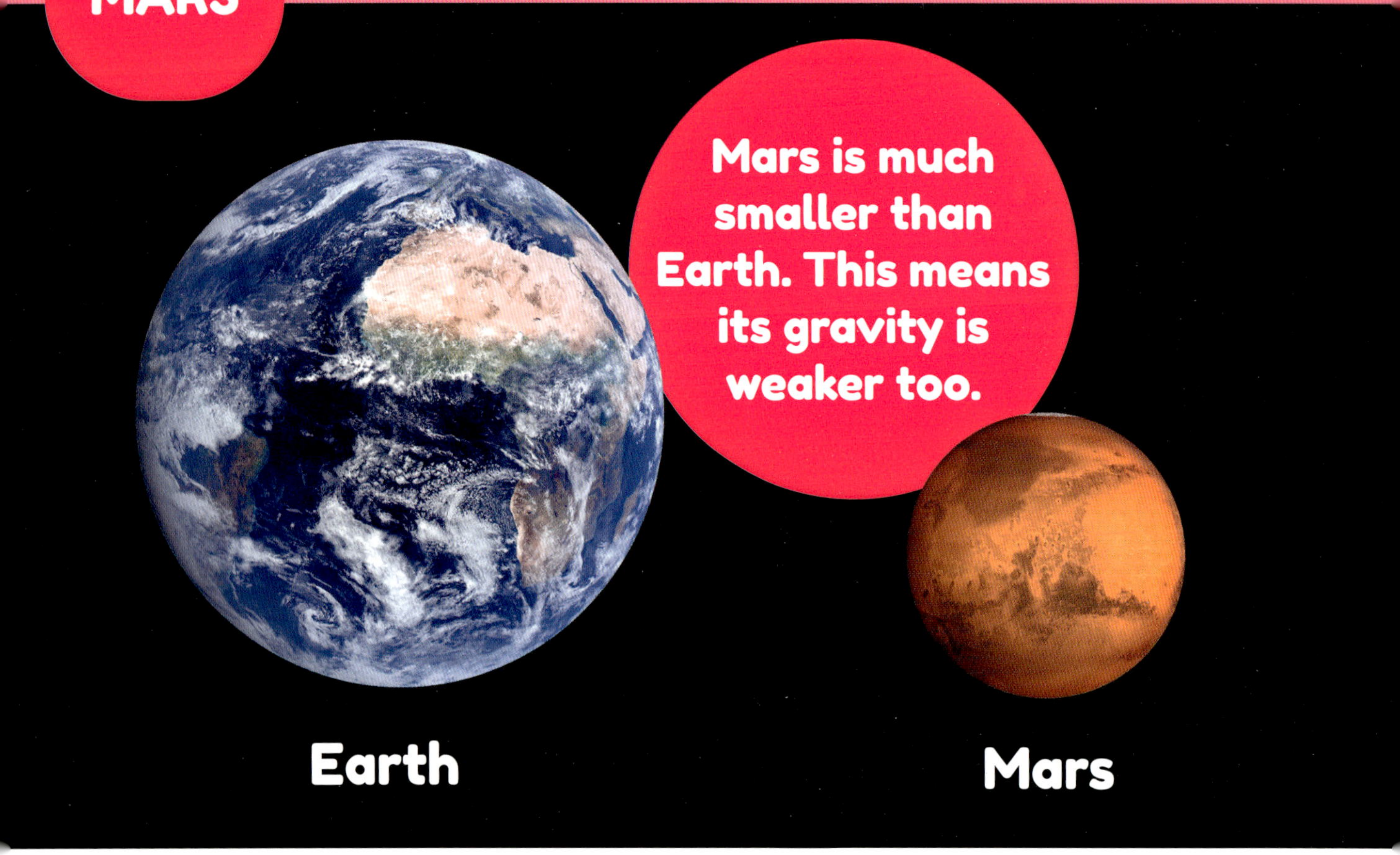

Mars is much smaller than Earth. This means its gravity is weaker too.
Earth
Mars

Planet Size

Mars is the second-smallest planet in the solar system. Only Mercury is smaller. Mars is about half as big across as Earth. It is also less dense than Earth.

FUN FACT!

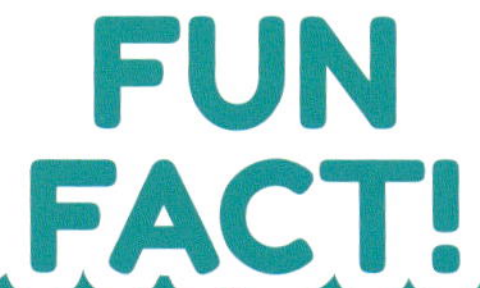

Mars has marsquakes, which are its form of earthquakes.

Structure

Mars is a terrestrial planet. Its dense core is made mostly of liquid iron. The core is surrounded by a rocky mantle. There is a crust over that. Volcanoes may still be active under Mars's surface. There may be water deep down too.

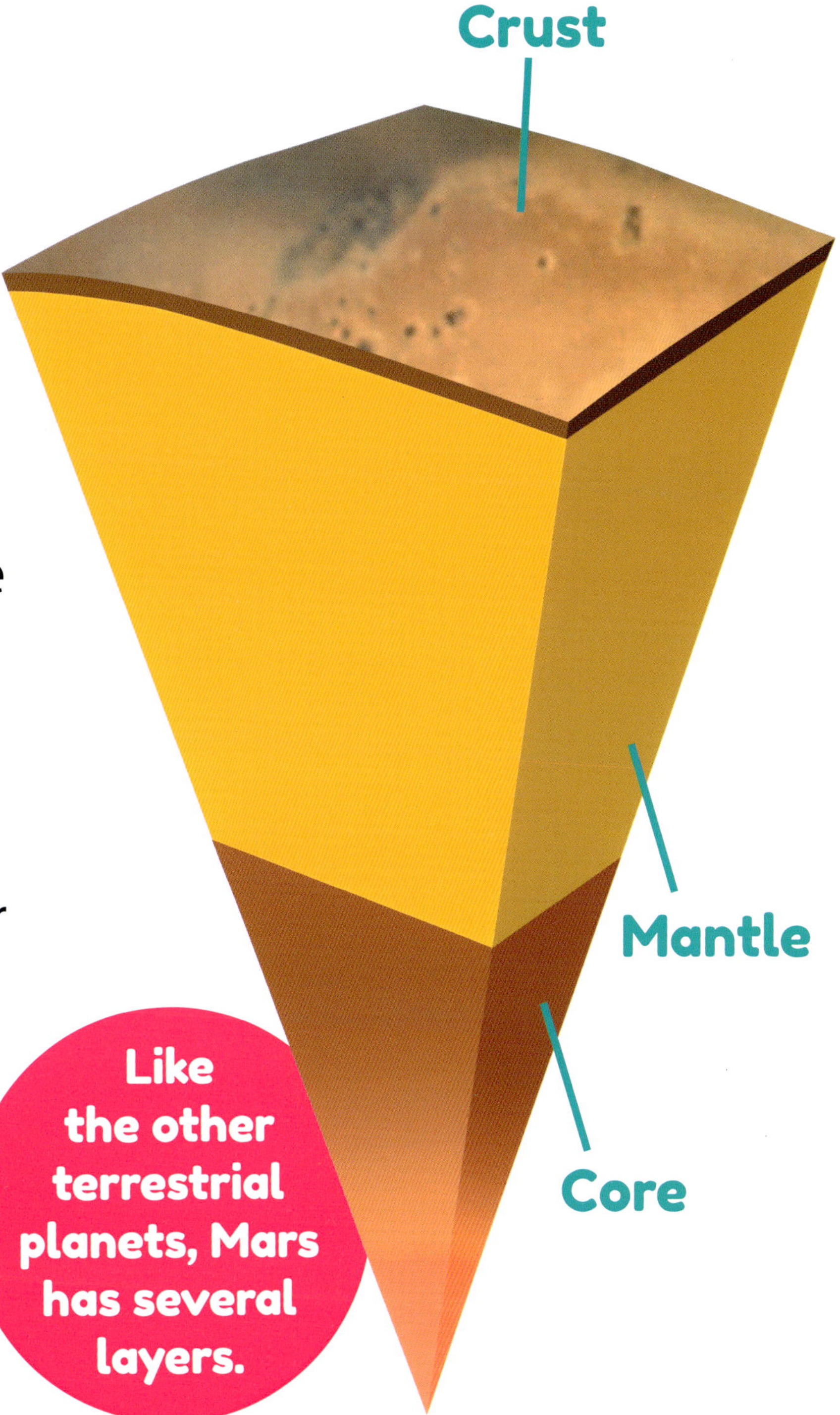

Like the other terrestrial planets, Mars has several layers.

Atmosphere

The atmosphere on Mars is very thin. Mars's atmosphere is also full of reddish dust. Carbon dioxide is the most common gas. There is very little oxygen. People could not breathe there.

Mars has little air, but spacecraft have seen blowing dust on the surface.

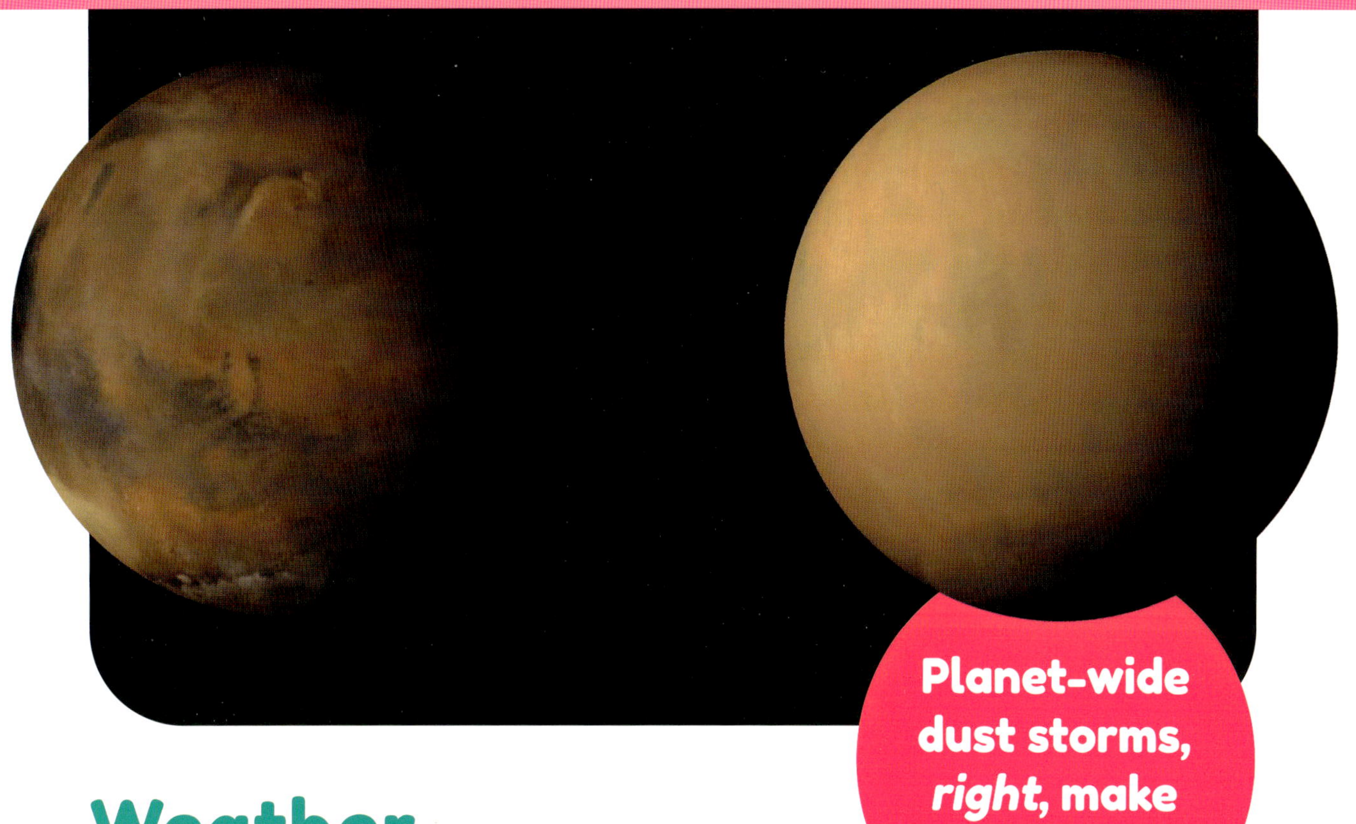

Planet-wide dust storms, *right*, make Mars look hazy.

Weather

Strong winds stir up dust storms on Mars. Sometimes these storms grow huge. They circle the whole planet. Temperatures can dip down to –225 degrees Fahrenheit (–143°C). They can rise to 70 degrees Fahrenheit (21°C).

Snowcubes

Carbon dioxide snow sometimes falls on Mars. Each flake is tinier than a hair. The flakes are shaped like cubes.

The mountain Olympus Mons is the size of the country of Poland.

On the Surface

Mars has the highest mountain in the solar system. It also has the largest canyon. Mars's poles are covered with ice. But most of the planet looks like a dry desert. Mars's rusty color comes from iron. This element is found in rocks and dust.

Moons

Mars has two small moons. They do not have enough gravity to be round. They are shaped more like potatoes. Phobos is larger. Deimos is smaller and farther away.

Why Explore Mars?

Mars was likely once warmer and wetter. People wonder if life existed there in the past. Exploring Mars may lead to answers.

Artists make images of what Mars could look like with water.

Mars Missions

More than 40 missions have headed for Mars. About half have failed. *Mariner 4* flew by in 1965. In 1976, *Viking 1* landed there. More recently, several rovers have explored the planet. Scientists are studying how to land humans on Mars. This will be a very challenging mission.

Jupiter has swirling bands of clouds.

Fifth from the Sun

Jupiter is the first outer planet. It is fifth from the sun. On average, it is 484 million miles (779 million km) away from the sun. Sunlight takes 43 minutes to reach it.

How Jupiter Got Its Name

Jupiter can be seen with the naked eye. Early people were able to track it in the sky. It was named long ago. Jupiter was the Roman god of the sky. He was also king of the gods.

Tracking Jupiter

Experts have studied tablets from more than 2,000 years ago. They show that the Babylonians tracked Jupiter using math. These people lived in what is now Iraq.

Orbit

The outer planets are very far from the sun. That means their orbits have to cover much more distance. It takes Jupiter about 12 Earth years to orbit the sun.

Jupiter is more than five times farther from the sun than Earth is.

Jupiter's speedy rotation leaves the planet slightly squished.

Rotation

Jupiter has the solar system's shortest day. The planet rotates in just under ten hours. The fast spin makes its middle wider. The poles flatten. Jupiter is almost straight on its axis. It does not have seasons.

Jupiter has more than twice the mass of all the other planets combined.

Planet Size

Jupiter is the biggest planet in the solar system. The others could all fit inside it. If Jupiter were a basketball, Earth would be a grape.

Structure

Jupiter is a gas giant. It has no surface. It is mostly a ball of gas. The main gas is hydrogen. There is also helium. Temperatures grow very hot near Jupiter's core. Pressure increases. The hydrogen turns into a liquid.

Scientists think Jupiter's core is made of ice, rock, and metal.

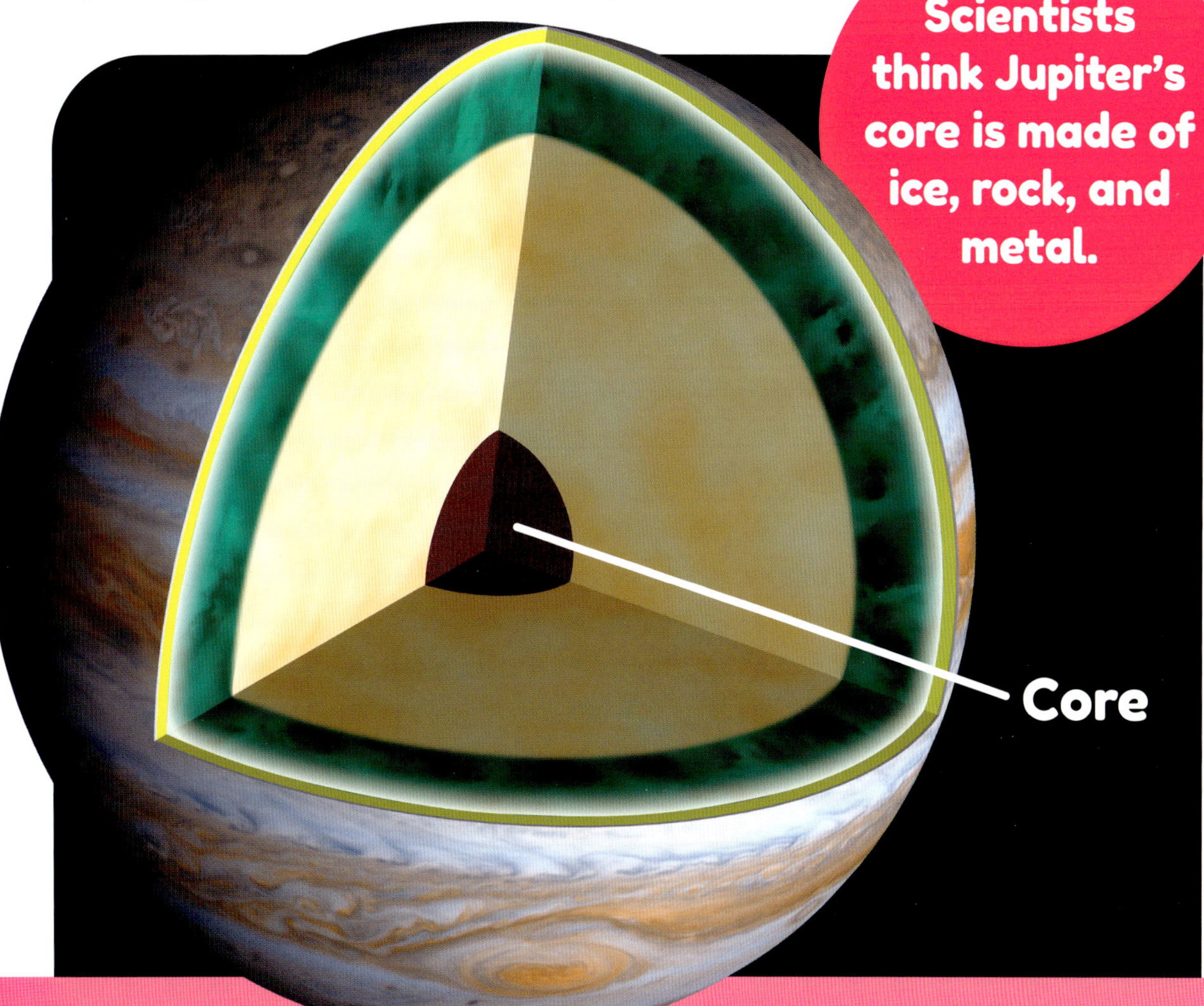

Atmosphere

Jupiter's atmosphere has layers. It is very thick. The planet is circled by dark and light bands. From space, Jupiter looks as if it has stripes. These are clouds. The bands change over time.

The *Juno* spacecraft took this photo of Jupiter's clouds. Scientists changed the colors to make features easier to see.

The Great Red Spot is the largest storm in the solar system.

Weather

Jupiter can be very cold. It can also be very hot. It depends on the atmosphere layer. The planet is windy and stormy. One huge storm is called the Great Red Spot. It is wider than Earth. Its clouds spin faster than 400 miles per hour (644 km/h).

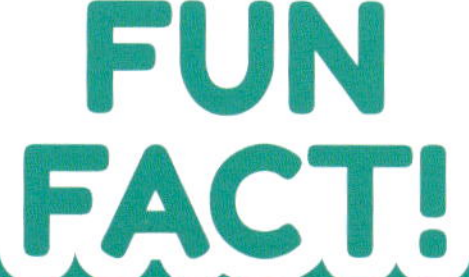

Scientists believe the Great Red Spot has lasted at least 300 years.

A space telescope caught a view of Jupiter's faint rings.

Jupiter's Rings

The outer planets all have rings. This includes Jupiter. Its rings are made mostly of dust. They are dark and hard to see. They were not discovered until 1979.

Moons

Jupiter had 95 official moons in 2024. More are likely to be discovered. Its moon Ganymede is the largest in the solar system. Callisto, Io, and Europa are other big moons. Most of Jupiter's other moons are much smaller.

Europa has a smooth surface with many lines running across it.

Why Explore Jupiter?

Jupiter is the solar system's oldest planet. Studying it gives scientists important information. They learn about planet creation. They see how solar systems form.

***Galileo* studied Jupiter and its moons in the 1990s.**

Jupiter Missions

Several spacecraft have visited Jupiter. *Pioneer 10* flew by in 1973. In 1995, *Galileo* entered orbit. *Juno* began orbiting in 2016. *Europa Clipper* launched in 2024. It will go into orbit around Jupiter in 2030.

Europa Clipper launched on a Falcon Heavy rocket.

Looking for Life on Europa

- Europa is Jupiter's fourth-largest moon. There may be an ocean under its icy crust.
- Scientists believe Europa might be able to support life under its surface.
- *Europa Clipper* will closely study the moon. The spacecraft is about as long as a basketball court.

Jupiter

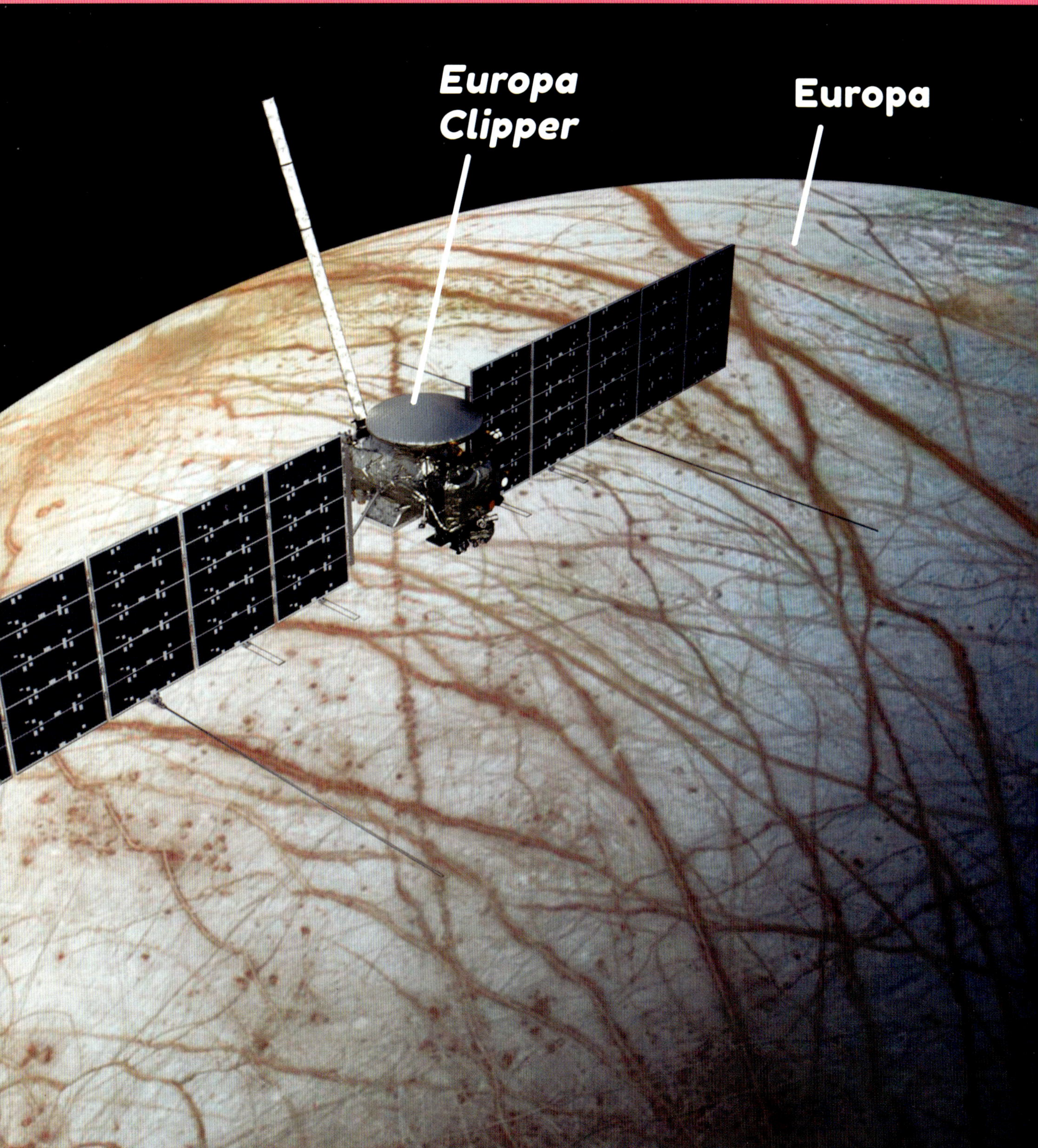
Europa
Clipper
Europa

With its large rings, Saturn looks unlike any other planet.

Sixth from the Sun

The ringed Saturn is the solar system's sixth planet. It averages 886 million miles (1.4 billion km) away from the sun. Sunlight takes 80 minutes to reach Saturn. Its neighbors are Jupiter and Uranus.

How Saturn Got Its Name

Saturn can be seen without a telescope. Long ago, it was named after a Roman god. He was the god of farming. He was also Jupiter's father.

Saturn is the farthest planet discovered in ancient times.

Saturn and Jupiter sometimes move close together. They can be seen side by side in the night sky.

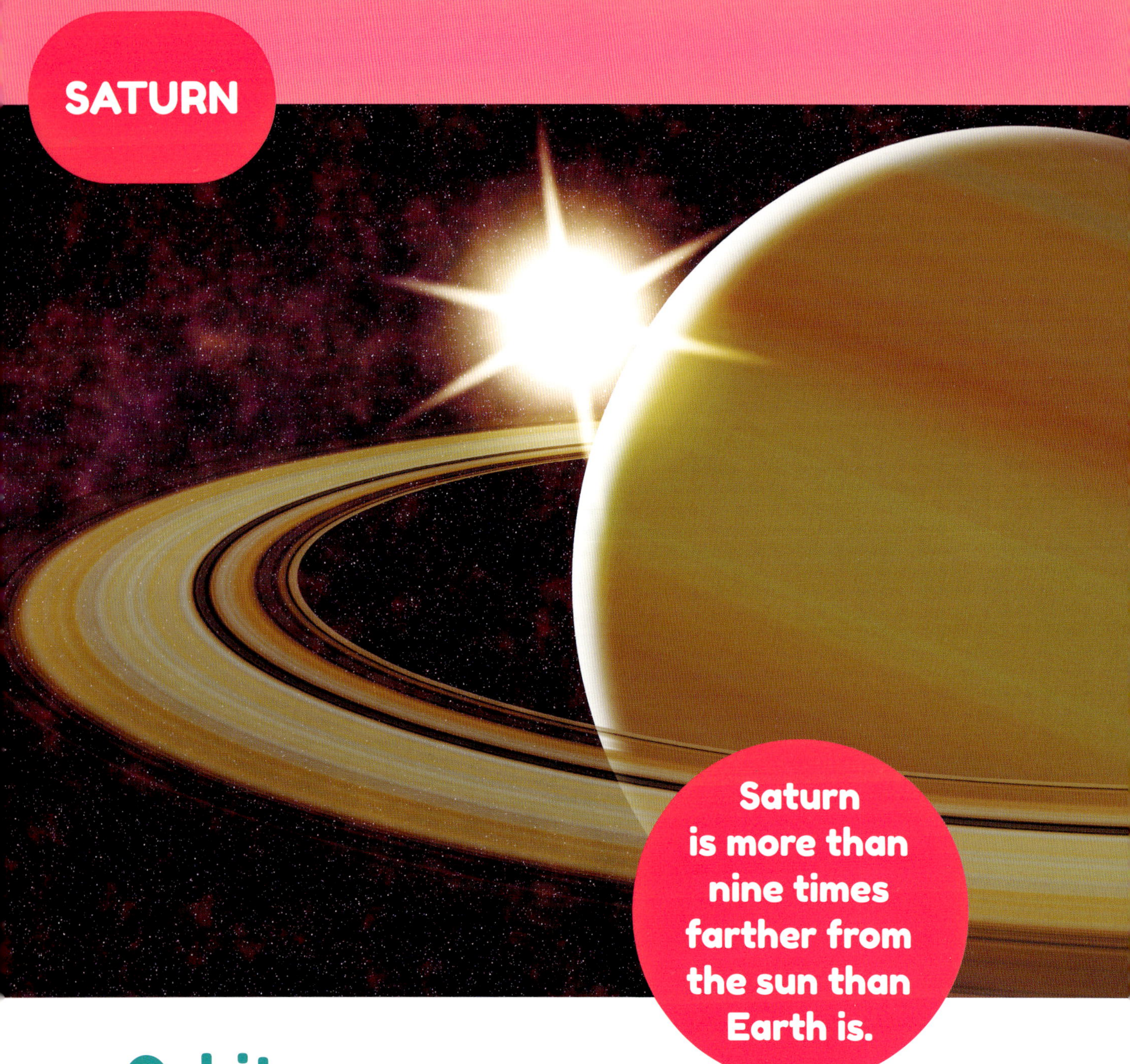

Saturn is more than nine times farther from the sun than Earth is.

Orbit

Saturn orbits far beyond Jupiter. Its orbit takes it on a long path around the sun. Completing one orbit takes more than 29 Earth years.

Rotation

A day on Saturn is very short. The planet rotates in just over ten and a half hours. This fast rotation makes it widen at its middle. It flattens at its poles. Like Earth, Saturn is tilted. This means it has seasons.

Saturn rotates much more quickly than Earth.

Planet Size

Saturn is the second-biggest planet in the solar system. Only Jupiter is bigger. Saturn is much larger than third-place Uranus. If Saturn were a volleyball, Earth would be a nickel.

Would Saturn Float in Water?

Saturn is less dense than water. If there were a bathtub big enough, the planet would float!

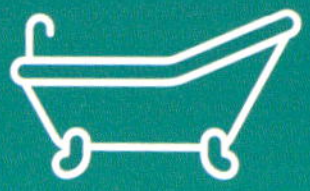

Saturn is smaller than Jupiter but bigger than Uranus and Neptune.

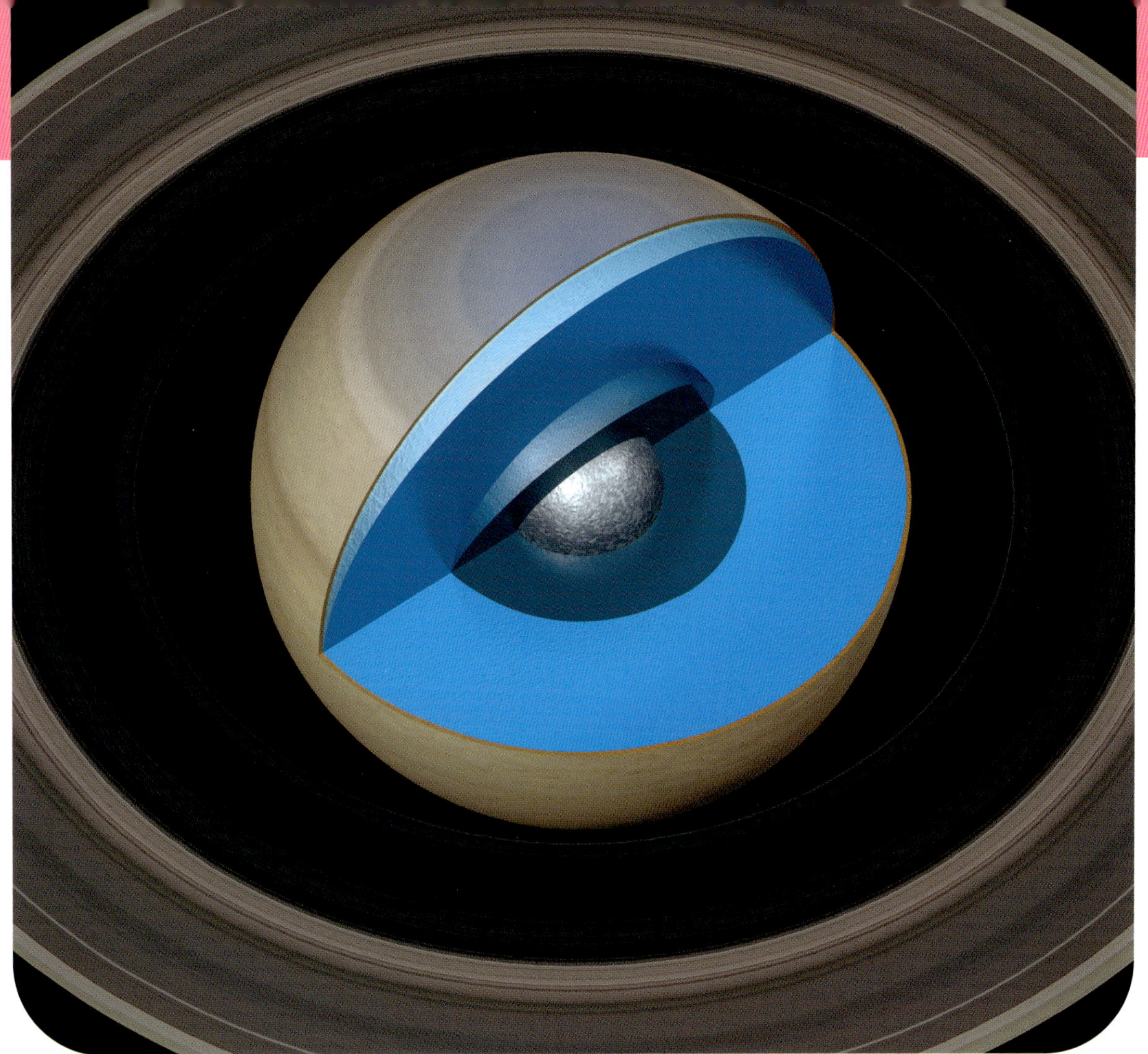

Saturn's layers hold hydrogen in gas and liquid forms.

Structure

Saturn's structure is similar to Jupiter's. It is a gas giant made mostly of hydrogen. It includes helium too. Deep inside the planet, the hydrogen becomes liquid.

Scientists study Saturn's shifting clouds.

Six-Sided Storm on Saturn

A hexagon-shaped cloud pattern surrounds Saturn's north pole. This huge storm was discovered in 1981. It is still there today.

Atmosphere

Saturn's thick atmosphere makes up most of the planet. Different layers of clouds blanket it. Like Jupiter, it has bands. But its stripes are not as bright.

Weather

Saturn's upper atmosphere is very cold. Temperatures are warmer closer to its hot core. Saturn is very windy. Wind speeds reach 1,100 miles per hour (1,800 km/h). Saturn has many huge storms. They can last a long time.

Saturn's north pole has a strange six-sided storm.

Saturn's Rings

All the gas giants have rings. Saturn's are the brightest. They are made of many pieces of ice and rock. Some pieces are as small as dust. A few are as big as houses. The rings are only about 30 feet (9 m) thick.

Viewed up close, Saturn's rings are not solid.

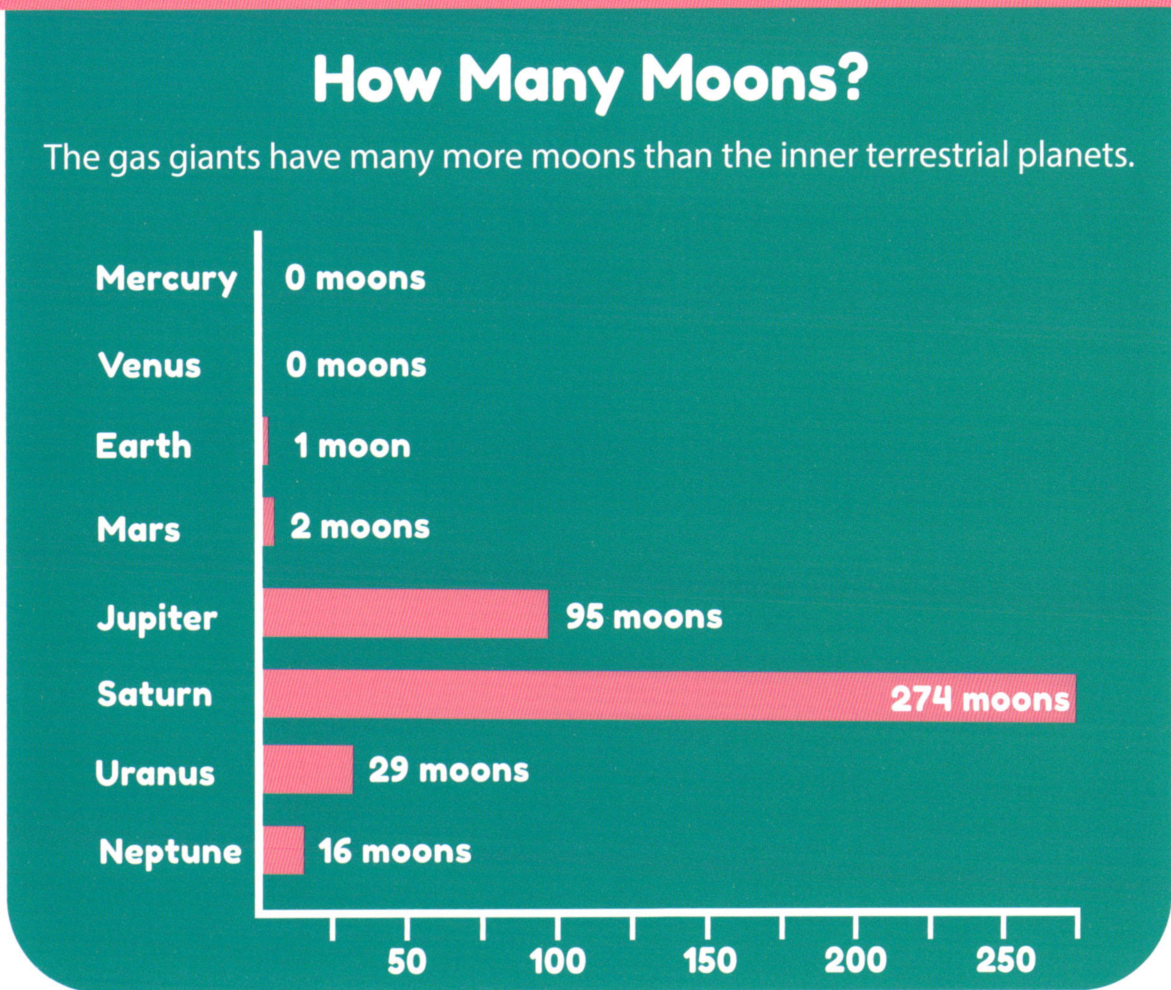

Moons

Saturn has the most moons of any solar system planet. In 2025, the count was 274. More may be discovered. Titan is its largest moon. It is the only moon with a thick atmosphere. The icy moon Enceladus has an underground ocean.

Why Explore Saturn?

Exploring Saturn teaches scientists about other gas giants. It helps them learn about how solar systems form. Scientists are also curious about Saturn's moons. They wonder if life could exist there.

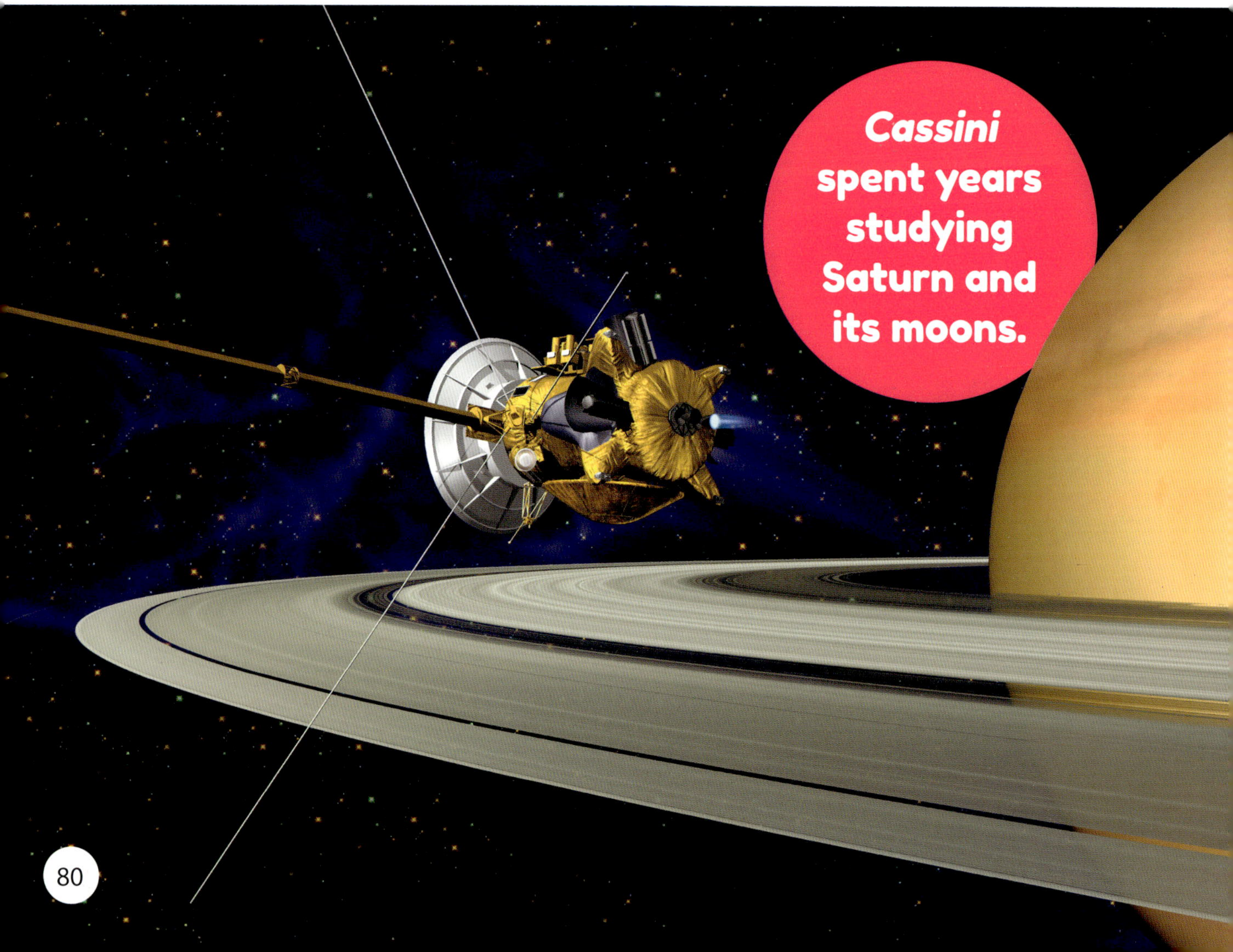

Cassini **spent years studying Saturn and its moons.**

Dragonfly is a flying drone that will explore Titan.

Saturn Missions

Four missions have visited Saturn. *Pioneer 11* was the first to fly by in 1979. *Cassini* orbited from 2004 to 2017. *Cassini* dropped the *Huygens* probe on Titan too. *Dragonfly* is planned for a 2034 landing on the hazy moon.

How Do You Say Uranus?

People are often unsure how to pronounce this planet's name. But scientist Emily Lakdawalla has an easy answer. Just say "You're a nuss!"

Seventh from the Sun

Uranus is the solar system's seventh planet. On average, it is 1.8 billion miles (2.9 billion km) from the sun. Sunlight takes two hours and 40 minutes to reach it. The planet's neighbors are Saturn and Neptune.

Uranus has fewer visible features than Jupiter and Saturn.

How Uranus Got Its Name

Uranus is hard to see with the naked eye. Early people did not know it was a planet. In 1781, William Herschel found Uranus with a telescope. Scientists soon realized it was a planet. A name was chosen. Uranus was the Greek god of the sky.

William Herschel worked alongside his sister, Caroline.

URANUS

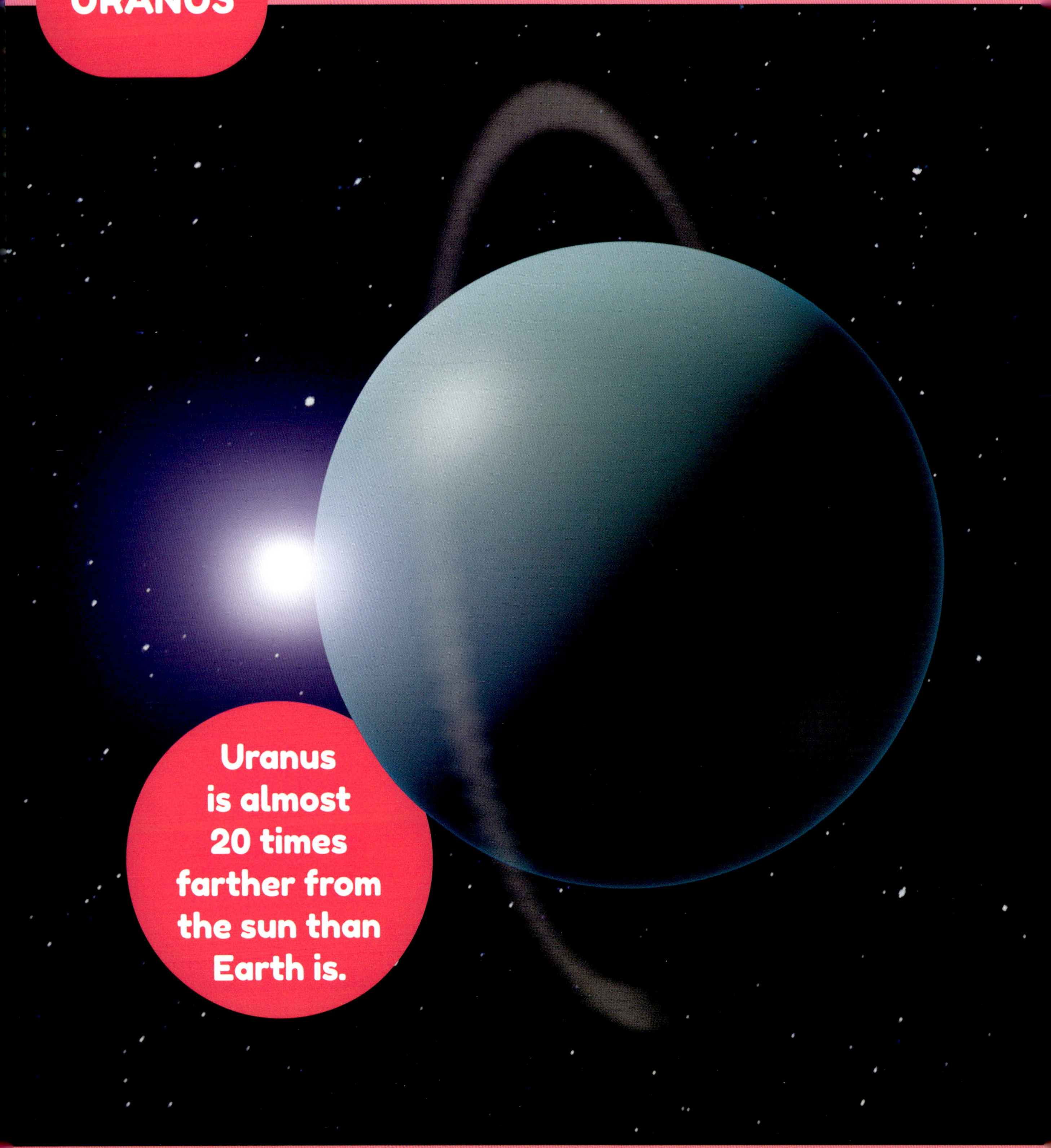

Uranus is almost 20 times farther from the sun than Earth is.

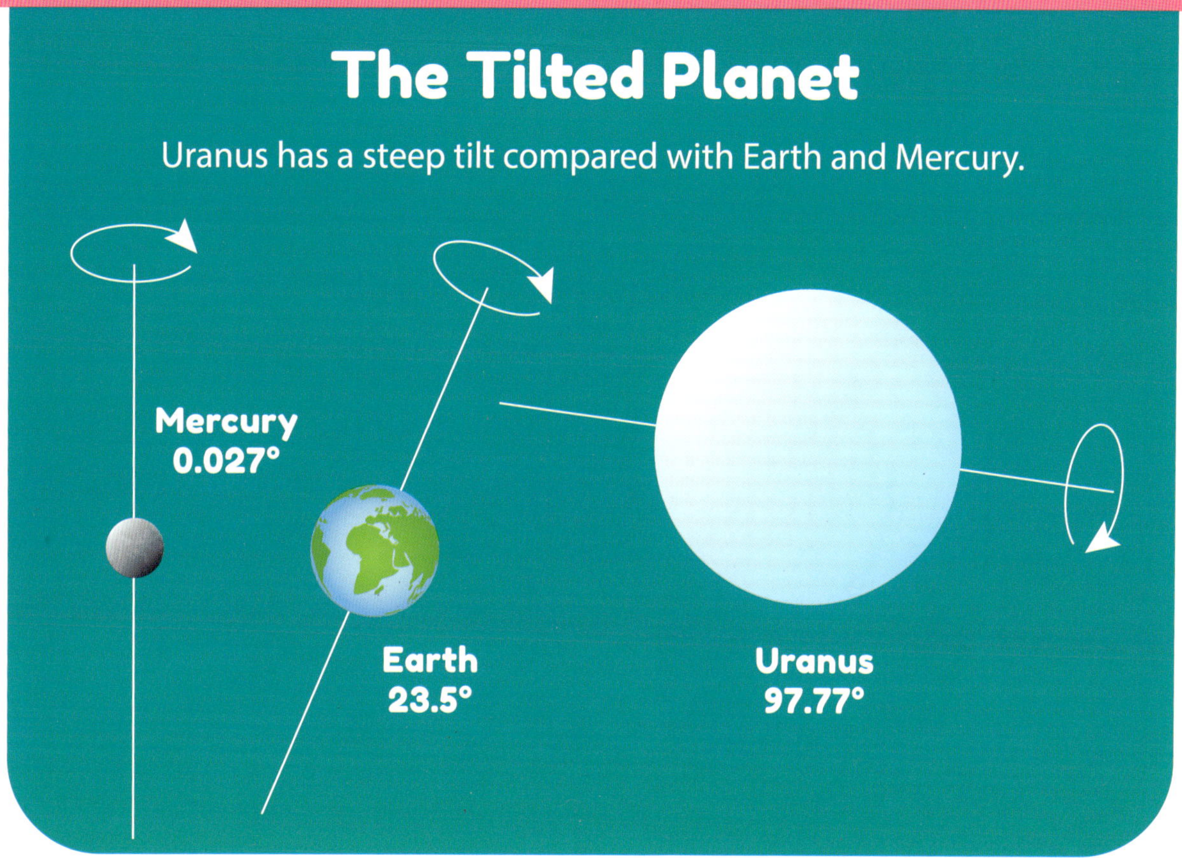

Orbit

Uranus's orbit is about 84 Earth years. It orbits on its side. It is the only solar system planet to do this.

Rotation

Uranus rotates in the opposite direction of most solar system planets. A Uranus day lasts just over 17 hours. The planet's tilt gives it seasons.

Planet Size

Uranus is the third-biggest planet in the solar system. It is slightly larger than Neptune. The ice giants are much smaller than the gas giants. But they are much bigger than the terrestrial planets.

FUN FACT!

Uranus has more than 14 times the mass of Earth.

Uranus is four times wider than Earth.

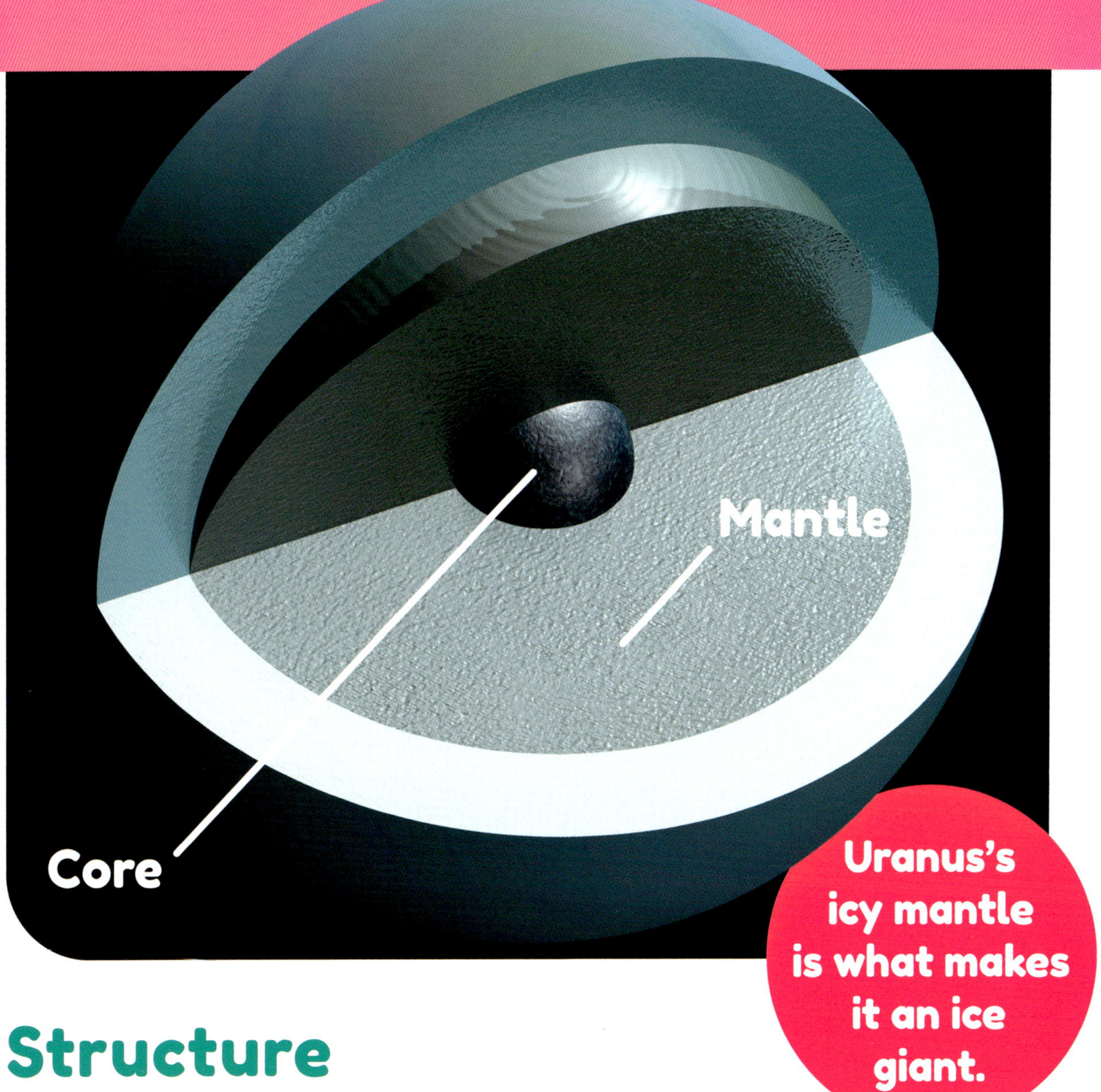

Uranus's icy mantle is what makes it an ice giant.

Structure

Uranus is an ice giant. Scientists believe it may have a small core. Around that may be a large, slushy mantle. The mantle is made of water, methane, and ammonia. They form a type of hot, dense ice. Uranus has no solid surface.

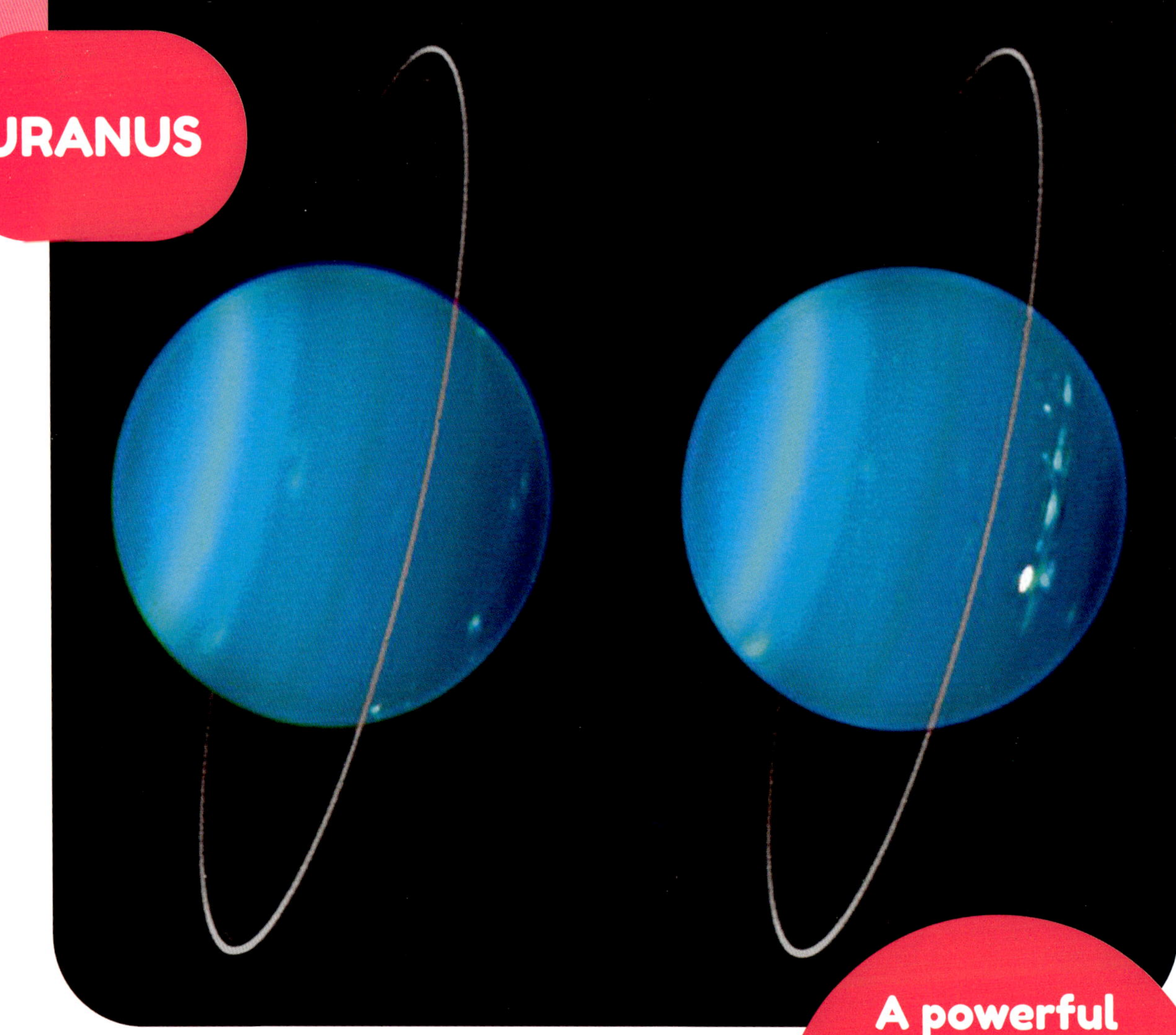

A powerful Earth-based telescope captured images of Uranus's two sides.

Atmosphere

Uranus has a thick, hazy atmosphere. It is also very cold. The atmosphere has layers. The top layer is mostly methane ice clouds. This gives Uranus its blue-green color. Much of the atmosphere is hydrogen and helium.

Weather

Uranus is a very windy planet. Winds can blow up to 560 miles per hour (900 km/h). Uranus is the coldest planet in the solar system. It has been measured at –371 degrees Fahrenheit (–224°C).

Uranus's Rings

Uranus has faint rings. They reflect less light than Saturn's rings. They were not discovered until 1977.

Uranus has 13 known rings.

Moons

Uranus has 29 small moons. More may be discovered. Some of the moons are tilted like their planet. Uranus's four largest moons are Titania, Oberon, Umbriel, and Ariel. Scientists believe there may be oceans under their surfaces.

Titania is Uranus's largest moon.

Why Explore Uranus?

Uranus is far from Earth. It is hard to explore. But scientists hope to learn more about its strange features. They want to learn more about ice giants. Many planets in the universe are similar. Studying Uranus helps scientists learn about these planets.

Uranus Mission

Voyager 2 is the only spacecraft to explore Uranus. It approached the planet in 1986. It took nine years to get there from Earth. Scientists are planning future missions. Until then, they study the planet in other ways. That includes using telescopes.

Voyager 2 **flew within 50,700 miles (81,600 km) of Uranus.**

Eighth from the Sun

Neptune is the solar system's eighth planet. It averages about 2.8 billion miles (4.5 billion km) from the sun. That is 30 times farther than Earth. It takes sunlight about four hours to reach Neptune.

Distance from the Sun

Long distances can be measured by how long it takes light to travel from one point to another. This chart shows how long it takes light to go from the sun to each planet.

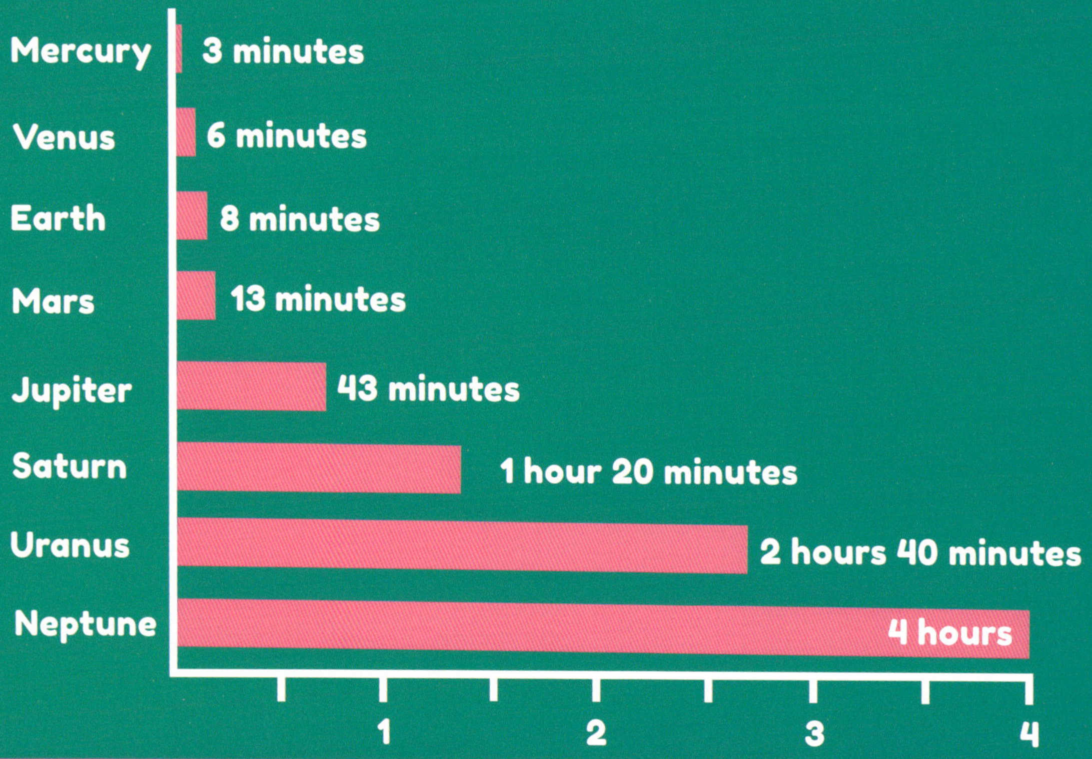

Planet	Time
Mercury	3 minutes
Venus	6 minutes
Earth	8 minutes
Mars	13 minutes
Jupiter	43 minutes
Saturn	1 hour 20 minutes
Uranus	2 hours 40 minutes
Neptune	4 hours

Axis: 1, 2, 3, 4

John Couch Adams figured out where to search for Neptune.

How Neptune Got Its Name

Uranus was discovered in 1781. But scientists later noticed its orbit was odd. Another planet's gravity might be pulling on the planet. They used this data to guess the unknown planet's location. When they searched this area with a telescope in 1846, they found Neptune. The planet was named for the Roman god of the sea.

NEPTUNE

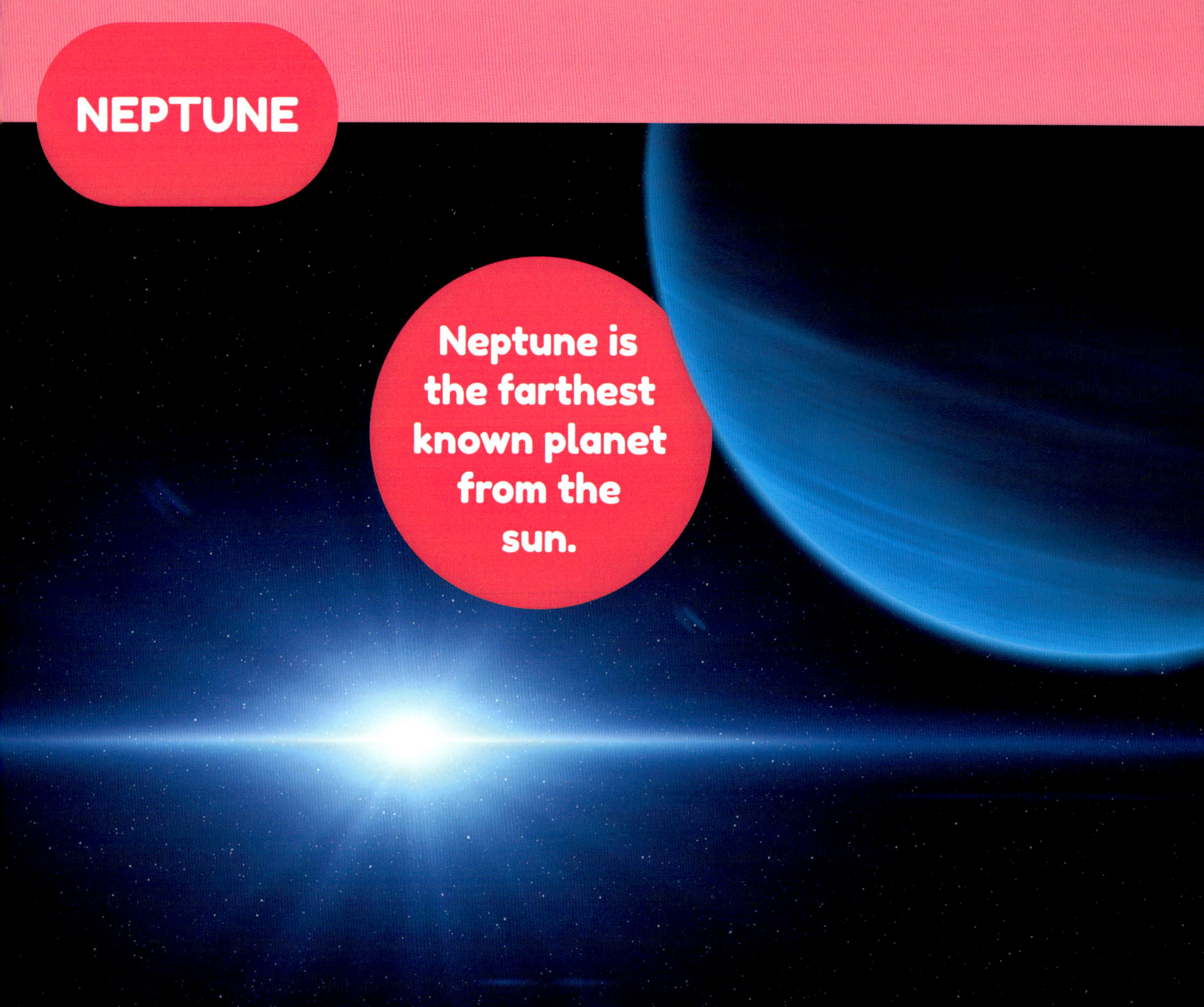

Orbit

It takes Neptune about 165 Earth years to orbit the sun. The planet has completed just one orbit since being discovered in 1846. This happened in 2011.

Rotation

Neptune rotates in about 16 hours. The planet is tilted on its axis. The tilt is similar to Earth's. Neptune has four seasons, as Earth does.

FUN FACT!

Neptune's seasons last more than 40 Earth years.

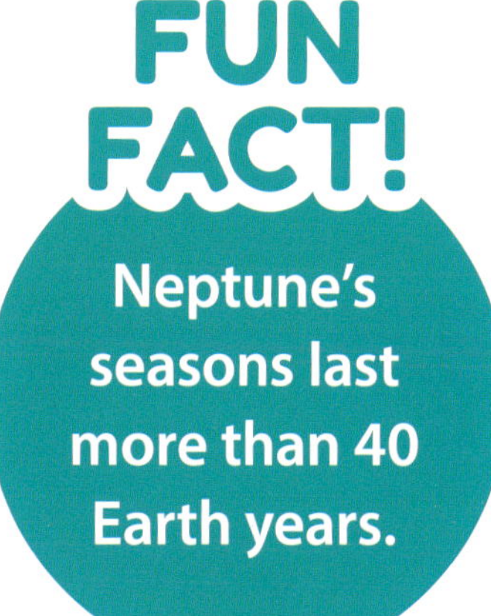

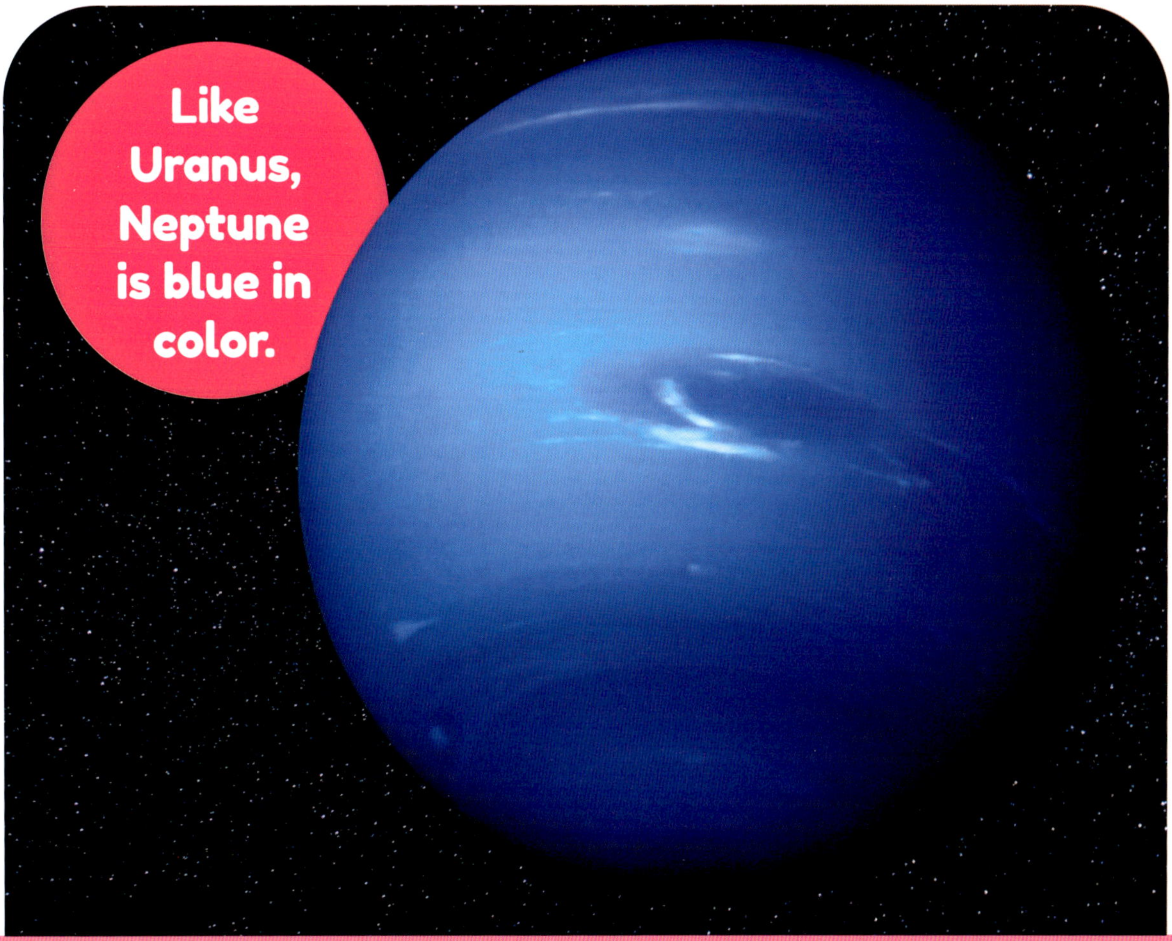

Like Uranus, Neptune is blue in color.

Planet Size

Neptune is the fourth-biggest solar system planet. It is slightly smaller than Uranus. It is about four times wider than Earth.

Neptune has about 17 times the mass of Earth.

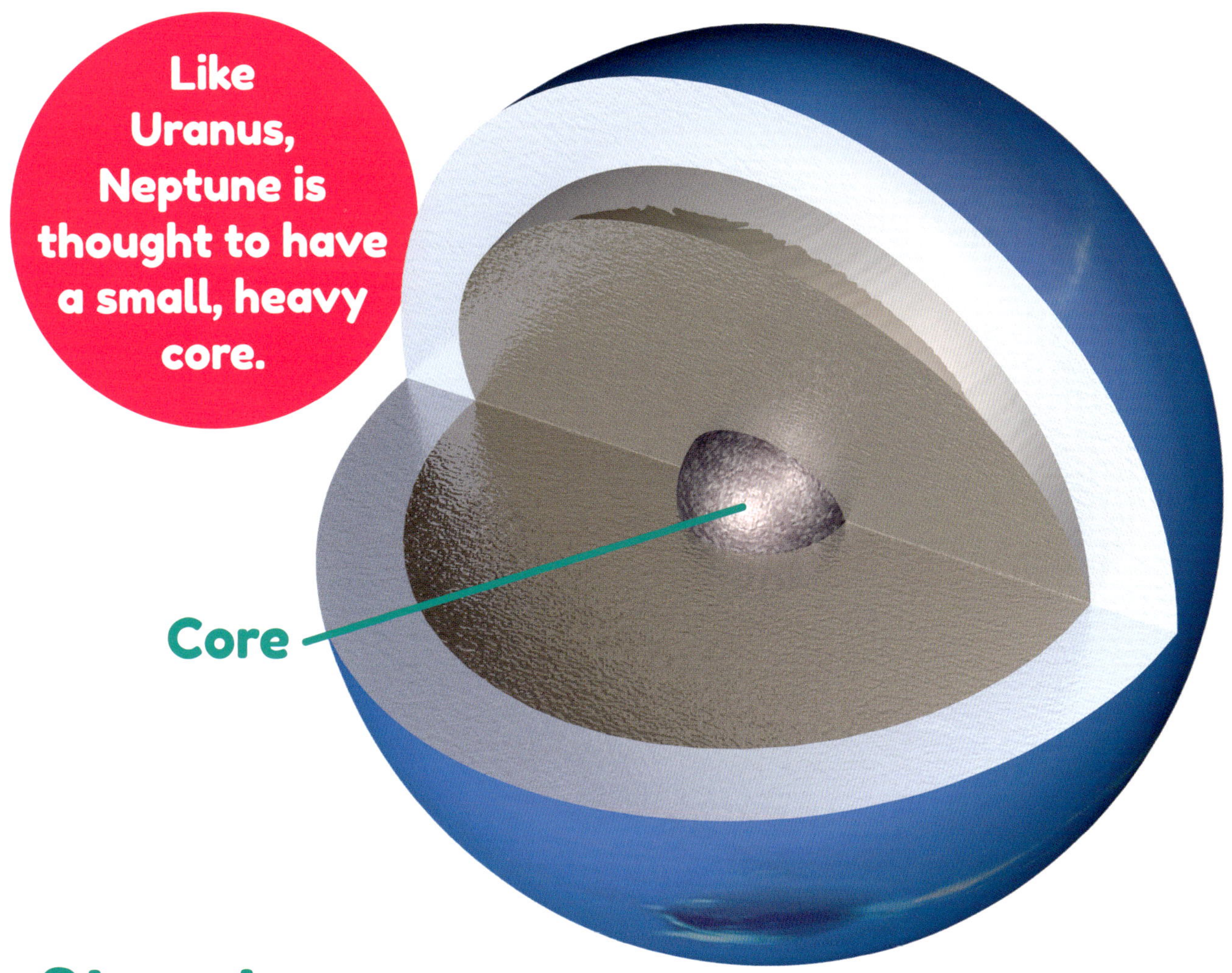

Structure

Neptune is an ice giant. It has a similar structure to Uranus. Scientists believe it may have a solid core. Most of the planet is water, methane, and ammonia. They form a kind of slushy ice. Neptune has no solid surface.

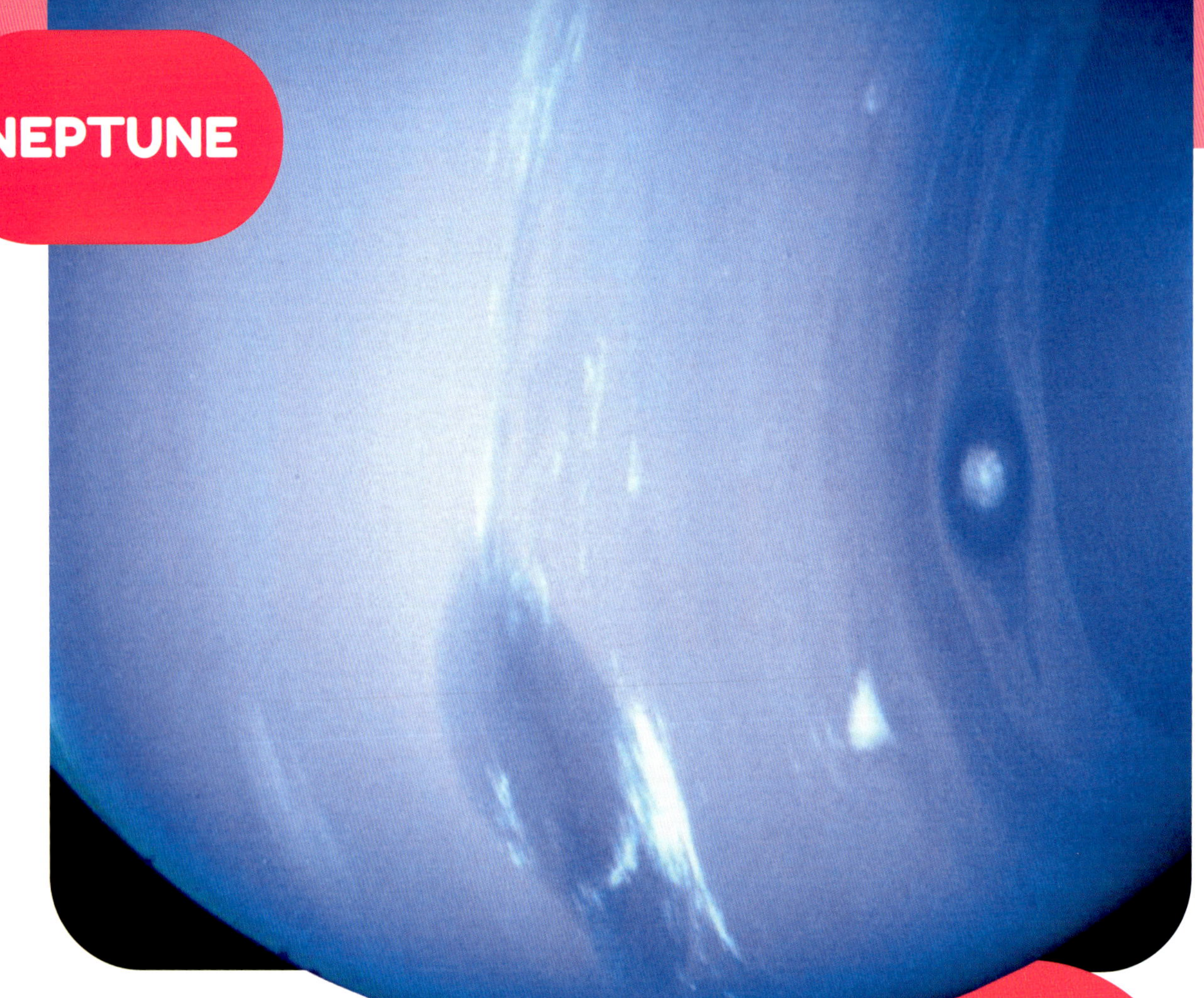

Neptune's clouds are always shifting.

Atmosphere

Neptune and Uranus are a lot alike. Neptune's thick atmosphere is covered by changing clouds. Its atmosphere is mostly hydrogen and helium. There is also a little methane. The methane gives Neptune its blue color.

Weather

The sun looks very dim from Neptune. The planet is dark and cold. It averages about –330 degrees Fahrenheit (–200°C). It is very windy. It also has big storms.

The Windiest World

Neptune is the windiest solar system planet. Winds can reach speeds of more than 1,200 miles per hour (1,900 km/h).

Neptune's Rings

Neptune has faint rings. They are hard to see. Its ring system also has arcs. These are clumps of dust. Scientists would expect the clumps to spread out. But they do not.

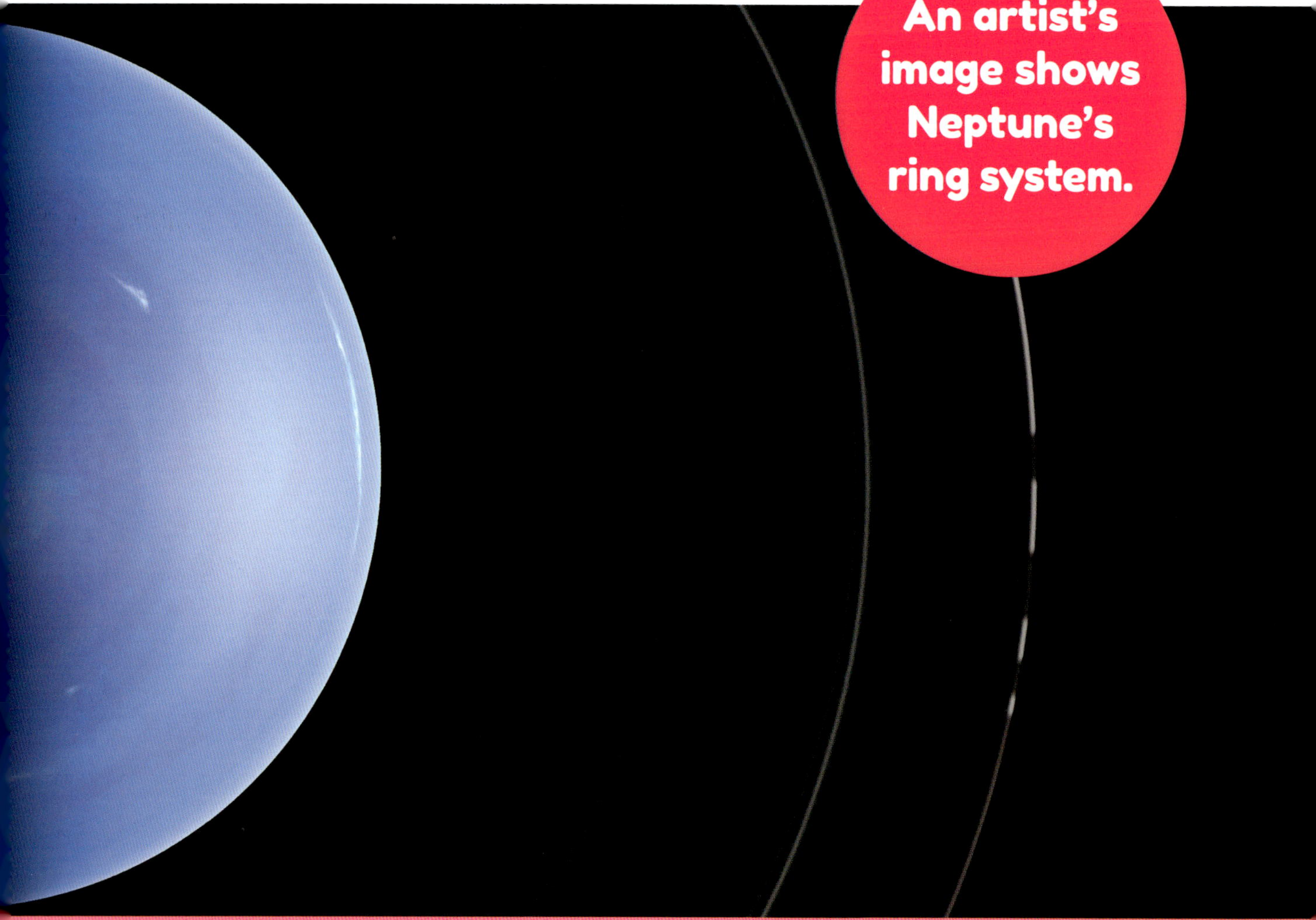

An artist's image shows Neptune's ring system.

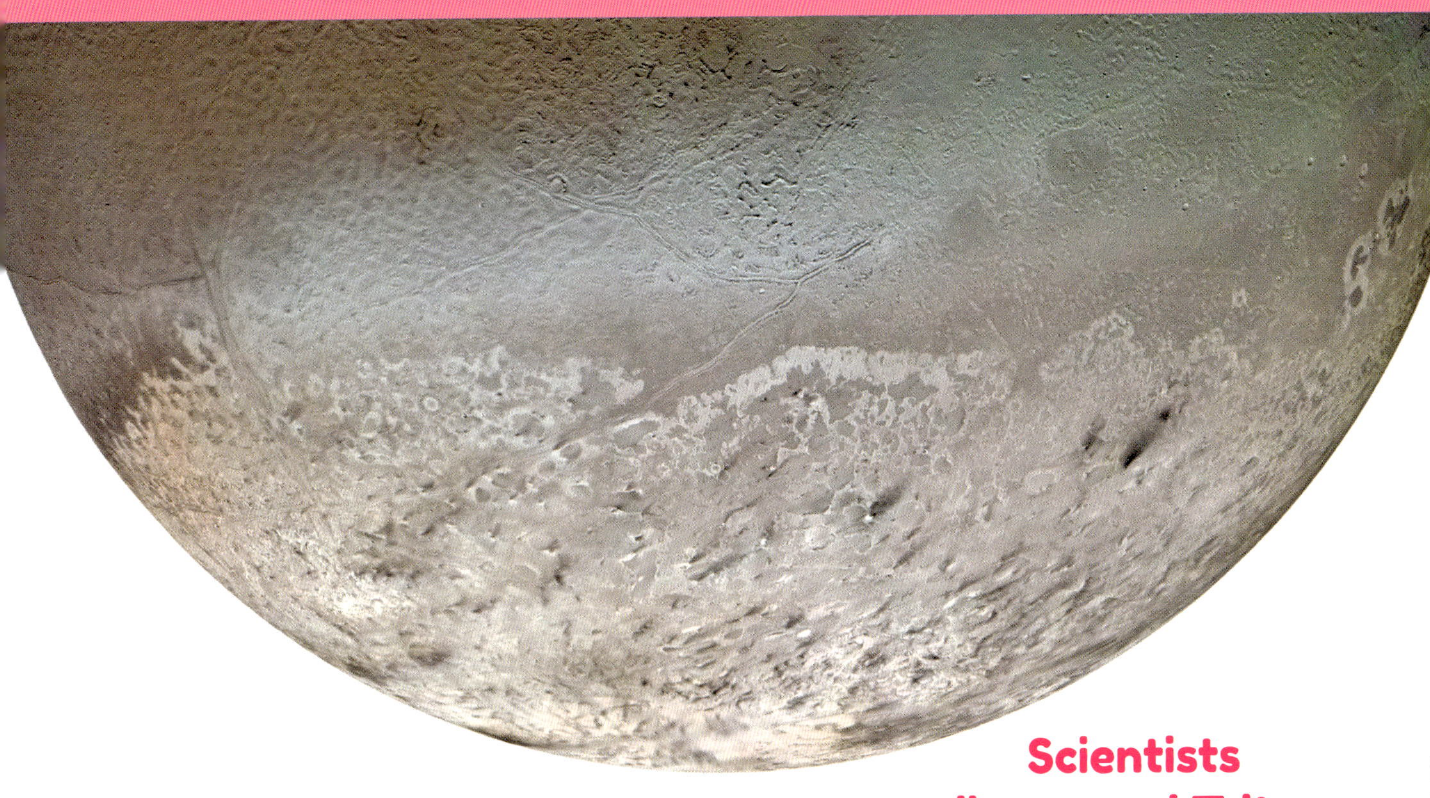

Scientists discovered Triton just a few weeks after Neptune.

Moons

Neptune has 16 known moons. More may be discovered. Triton is its largest moon. Triton has an odd orbit. It orbits Neptune in the opposite direction of Neptune's rotation. No other large solar system moon orbits this way.

FUN FACT!

Triton may have been captured by Neptune's gravity, rather than forming along with the planet.

Why Explore Neptune?

Neptune is far from Earth. That makes it hard to explore. But several other planets in the universe are like it. Learning about Neptune helps scientists learn more about those worlds.

Neptune Missions

Voyager 2 is the only spacecraft to have visited Neptune. It flew by the planet in 1989. That was about 12 years after the probe left Earth. No other missions have been planned. Scientists study the planet using telescopes.

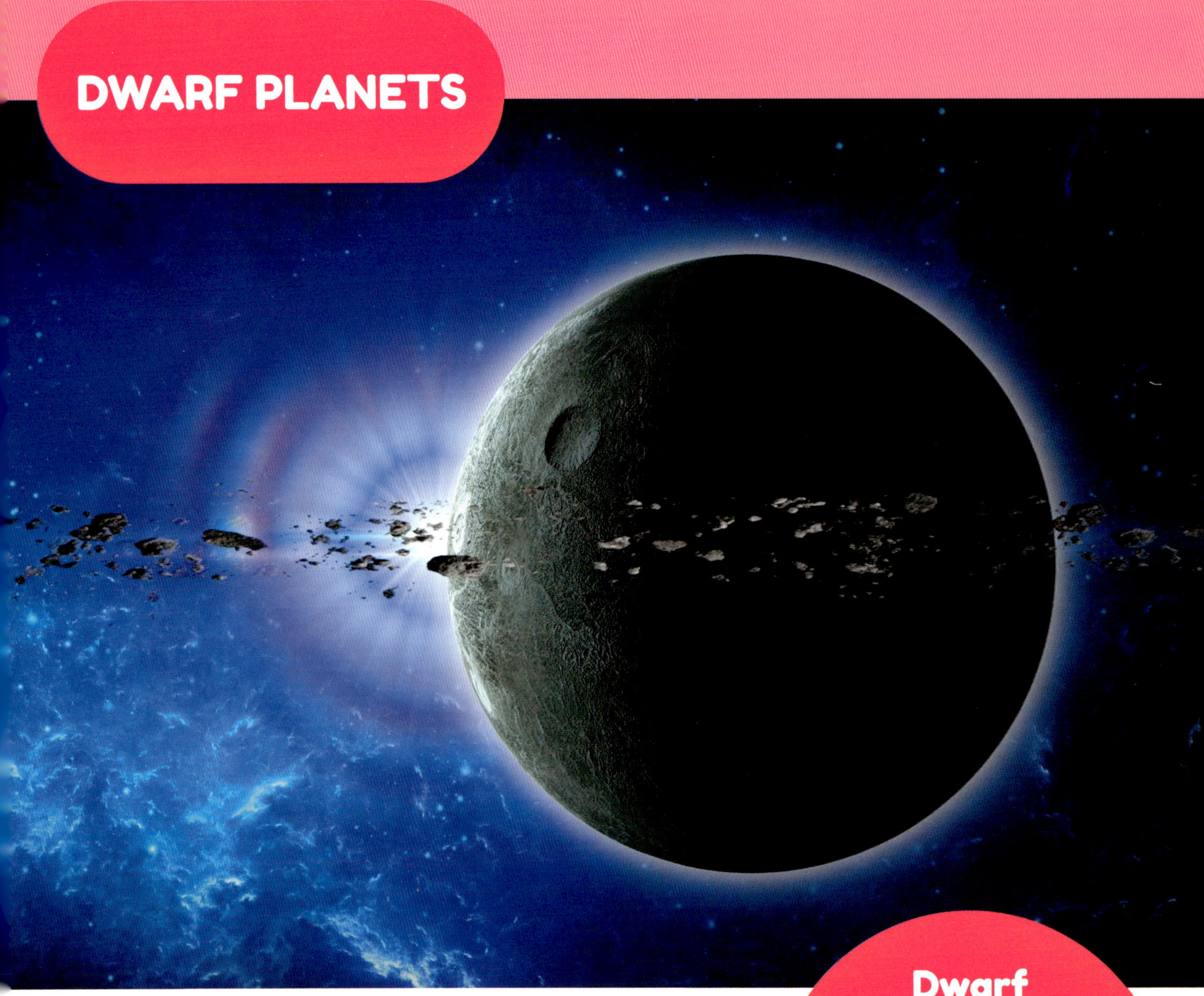

Dwarf planets are much smaller than the solar system's eight main planets.

What Is a Dwarf Planet?

Dwarf planets have some things in common with planets. They orbit the sun. They are mostly round. The solar system has five known dwarf planets. They are Pluto, Ceres, Haumea, Makemake, and Eris.

Different from Planets

Dwarf planets have important differences from planets. They are smaller and have less gravity. This means they cannot keep their orbit clear of other objects.

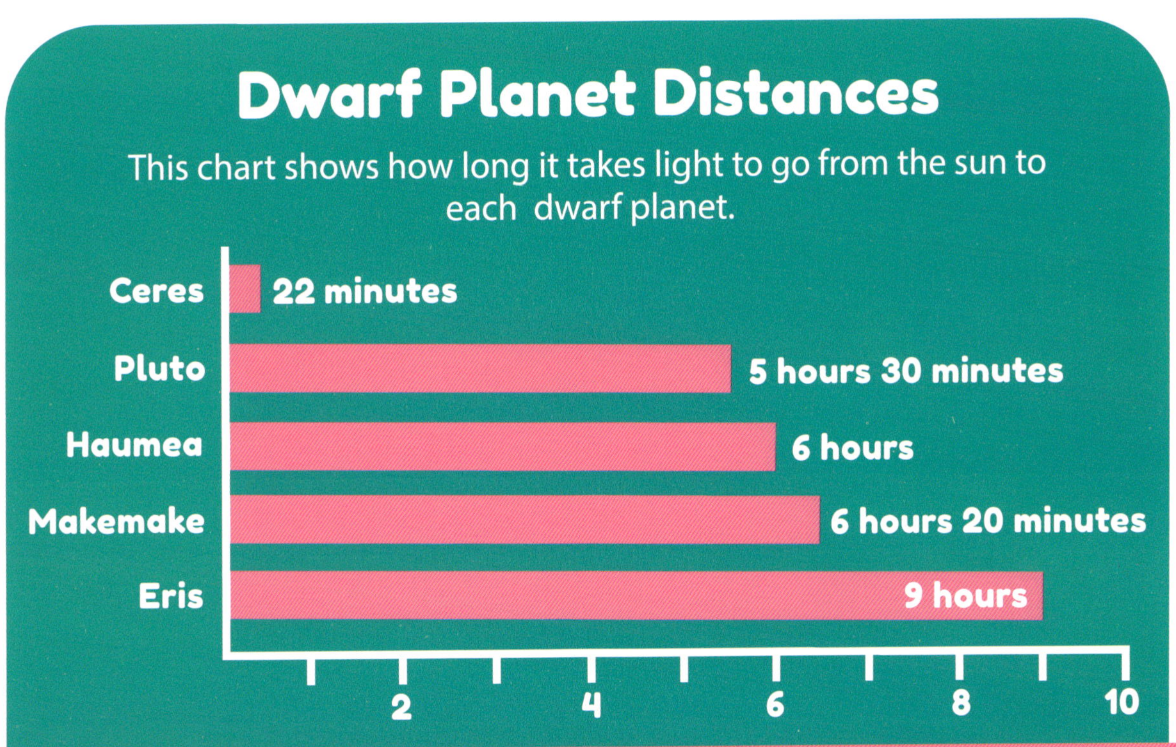

The Main Asteroid Belt

Asteroids orbit the sun. They are small, rocky objects. These objects often have odd shapes. They are left over from the early solar system. Most of them are in the main asteroid belt. This is between Mars and Jupiter.

FUN FACT!

There are millions of objects in the main asteroid belt. Ceres is the biggest.

The main asteroid belt includes objects of many different sizes.

The *Dawn* spacecraft took sharp photos of Ceres.

Ceres, the Dwarf Planet

Ceres is the smallest dwarf planet. It is in the main asteroid belt. It is the only dwarf planet located there. Ceres was once considered an asteroid.

The Kuiper Belt is beyond the orbit of Neptune.

The Kuiper Belt

The Kuiper Belt circles the outer solar system. It includes small space objects. These are more leftovers from the early solar system. The dwarf planets Pluto, Haumea, Makemake, and Eris are found there.

KBOs

KBO stands for Kuiper Belt Object. This is one name for the objects in this area. Scientists believe the Kuiper Belt has millions of KBOs. They are mostly made of ice. Neptune's gravity probably kept them from combining into a planet.

The Kuiper Belt has many small, icy objects.

Pluto

Pluto was discovered in 1930. It was called the ninth planet. But things changed in 2006. Scientists created the term *dwarf planet*. Pluto is now considered one of these instead. It does not have enough gravity to clear its orbit.

Pluto has a large heart-shaped feature on its surface.

Pluto's largest moon is named Charon.

A Distant World

Sunlight reaches Pluto in about five and a half hours. Pluto is about two-thirds the width of Earth's moon. It is the largest dwarf planet. Its orbit takes 248 Earth years. The orbit is very egg shaped. Sometimes Pluto is closer to the sun than Neptune is.

Dwarf Planet Moons

All the dwarf planets are smaller than Earth's moon. Some dwarf planets have moons of their own. Pluto has five.

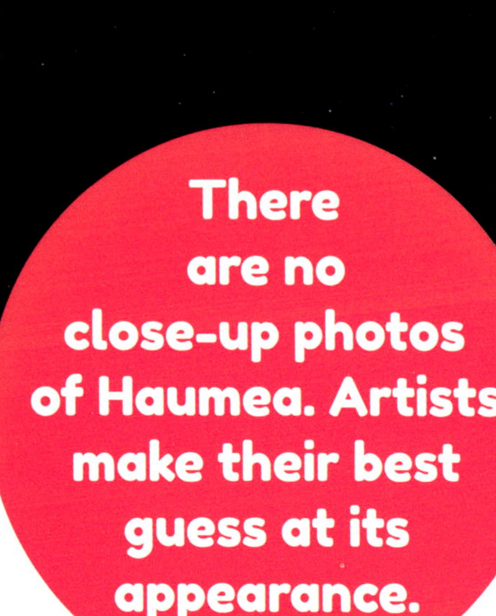

Haumea

Sunlight reaches Haumea in about six hours. It rotates in just four hours. This caused it to become shaped like a football. Haumea's orbit lasts about 285 Earth years. The dwarf planet has rings. It also has two moons.

Makemake

Sunlight takes more than six hours to reach Makemake. This dwarf planet travels around the sun in 305 Earth years. It is one of the Kuiper Belt's brightest objects. Scientists believe it has one moon.

Makemake may have a reddish-brown color.

Eris is about the size of Pluto.

Eris

Eris is the farthest known dwarf planet. Sunlight takes over nine hours to reach it. The dwarf planet takes 557 Earth years to orbit. It has a small moon.

Exploring the Dwarf Planets

The *Dawn* spacecraft orbited Ceres in 2015. *New Horizons* flew by Pluto in 2015. Scientists are planning future missions. They study dwarf planets from Earth. They use telescopes to search for more of these small worlds. There may be hundreds more to find.

Scientists made *New Horizons* to be small and fast. It still took nine years to reach Pluto.

Scientists do not know if Planet X is real.

What Is Planet X?

Some scientists think the solar system holds a surprise. They believe there is another planet. They think it is far past Neptune. They call it Planet 9. Some also call it Planet X.

Does Planet X Really Exist?

Scientists study many objects in the outer solar system. Their orbits are sometimes odd. So are their tilts. This makes scientists believe Planet X could be out there. They think its gravity might affect these other objects.

FUN FACT!

If Planet X is real, its orbit could take more than 10,000 Earth years.

The Closest Exoplanet

Proxima Centauri b is the closest known exoplanet. It is over four light-years away. That means it would take light four years to travel the distance.

What Are Exoplanets?

Exoplanets are planets outside the solar system. They were first seen in the 1990s. Scientists have found more than 5,800 of them. Many more are waiting to be discovered.

An exoplanet's effects on its star can reveal that it exists.

Finding Exoplanets

Exoplanets are dim and far away. Scientists use clever ways to find them. One is called the "wobble" method. Scientists notice a star making tiny movements. That can mean an exoplanet's gravity is pulling on it.

Exoplanets may have strange landscapes.

Types of Exoplanets

Some exoplanets are like solar system planets. But some are very different. There are gas giants much bigger than Jupiter. There are planets called mini-Neptunes. There are others called super-Earths.

Odd Exoplanets

Some exoplanets are very odd. One known exoplanet is bright pink. Another has storms that rain glass. Another one has the density of a marshmallow. Some exoplanets orbit two stars.

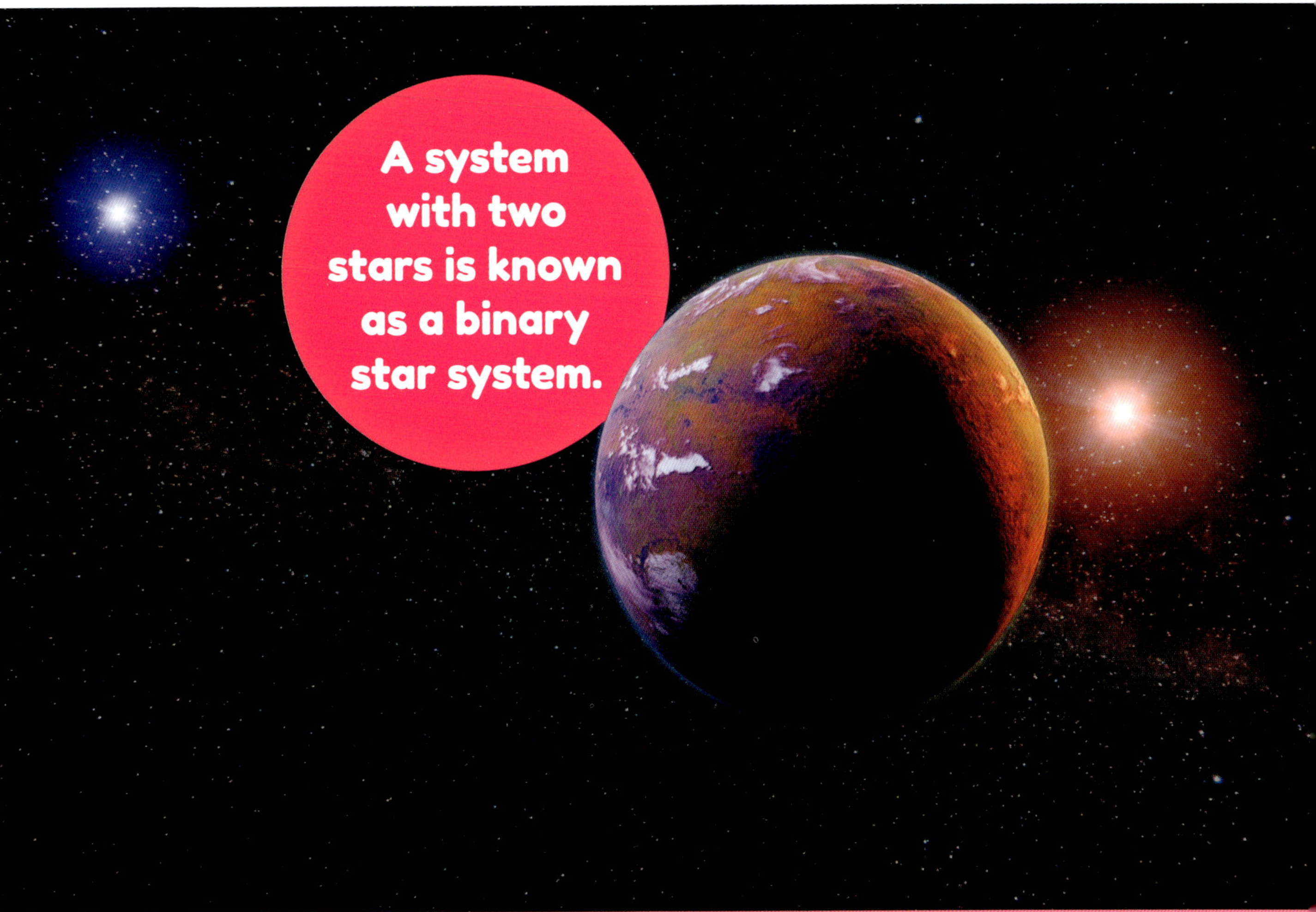

Why Study Exoplanets?

Scientists study exoplanets to better understand the solar system. They are also looking for planets that could support life. These planets would have to be at the right distance from their stars. Too close and they would be too hot. Too far away and they would be too cold.

A planet must be a certain distance from its star to have liquid water.

The James Webb Space Telescope will help scientists learn more about exoplanets.

Exoplanet Searchers

Huge telescopes continue the search for exoplanets. The Vera Rubin Observatory is in Chile. It started operating in 2025. Telescopes are also launched into space. The largest ever is the James Webb Space Telescope. It launched in 2021.

GLOSSARY

ammonia
A combination of nitrogen and hydrogen that has a strong smell.

atmosphere
The gases that surround an object in space.

axis
An invisible line that runs up and down through a planet's middle and that the planet spins around.

carbon dioxide
A gas made of carbon and oxygen.

clockwise
The direction in which a clock's hands rotate.

density
The amount of mass in a given volume.

exosphere
A very thin layer of gases around an object in space.

gravity
A force that objects have that pulls at other objects.

hazy
Cloudy.

helium
The second-lightest chemical element.

hydrogen
The lightest chemical element.

methane
A gas made of carbon and hydrogen.

mission
A task or job.

orbit
To follow a curved path around another object.

tilted
At an angle instead of straight.

TO LEARN MORE

More Books to Read

Borgert-Spaniol, Megan. *The Sun*. Abdo, 2026.

Stott, Carole. *Planets*. DK, 2023.

Venit, Katie. *Cassini's Mission: A Spacecraft, a Tiny Moon, and the Search for Life beyond Earth*. Candlewick, 2025.

Online Resources

To learn more about the planets, please visit **abdobooklinks.com** or scan this QR code. These links are routinely monitored and updated to provide the most current information available.

INDEX

PHOTO CREDITS

Cover Photos: Adobe Stock, front, back

Interior Photos: Shutterstock Images, 1, 3, 4 (top), 4 (bottom), 5, 6–7, 10, 12 (left), 12 (right), 16 (bottom), 20, 21, 24, 27, 29 (top), 29 (bottom), 34, 36, 39, 40, 41, 42, 44, 48, 51 (bottom), 53, 54, 56, 57 (bottom), 58, 70, 74 (top), 74 (bottom), 76 (bottom), 82 (top), 84, 86, 90, 92, 93, 96, 97, 98, 101 (top), 101 (bottom), 106, 108, 111, 113 (bottom), 116, 119, 120 (top), 123, 124; NASA, 8, 14, 15, 16 (top), 17, 18, 28, 31, 32, 38, 47, 50, 51 (top), 55, 59, 66, 67, 68–69, 76 (top), 80, 81, 91, 100, 103, 104, 109, 112, 113 (top), 116–117; Alan Dyer/VWPics/Alamy, 9; Chris Butler/Science Source, 11; Spencer Sutton/Science Source, 13; European Space Agency/Science Source, 19; Vadim Sadovski/Shutterstock Images, 22, 118; Red Line Editorial, 23, 79, 94, 107; Carlos Clarivan/Science Source, 25, 75, 87, 99; Mark Garlick/Science Source, 26, 46, 78, 102; Detlev van Ravenswaay/ Science Source, 30, 52, 83, 89; Max Belchenko/Shutterstock Images, 33; Ramil Gibadullin/Shutterstock Images, 35; Kateryna Kon/Science Source, 37; Raul Almu/Shutterstock Images, 43 (top); Eugene A. Cernan/NASA, 43 (bottom); AstroStar/Shutterstock Images, 45; Monica Schroeder/Science Source, 49; Alan Dyer/Stocktrek Images/Science Source, 57 (top); Marcel Clemens/Shutterstock Images, 60; Paul Wootton/Science Source, 61; Thomas Thomopoulos/NASA, 62; Kevin M. Gill/NASA, 63, 65, 77; Ricardo Hueso and Judy Schmidt/ESA/ Webb, 64; Damian Peach/Science Source, 71; Vink Fan/Shutterstock Images, 72; John Beetle/Shutterstock Images, 73; NASA Images/Shutterstock Images, 82 (bottom); Angela Cini/Shutterstock Images, 85; Lawrence Sromovsky/NASA, 88; Royal Astronomical Society/Science Source, 95; NASA/Science Source, 105; Nicolle R. Fuller/Science Source, 110; Diego Barucco/Shutterstock Images, 114, 115; Jurik Peter/Shutterstock Images, 120 (bottom), 121, 122; Dima Zel/ Shutterstock Images, 125